W9-BTF-610

KUMON MATH WORKBOOKS

Multiplication

Table of Contents

KUM⬤N

Level

Date / /

Name

Score /100

1 Add.

3 points per question

(1) $2 + 2 = 4$

(2) $3 + 3 = 6$

(3) $7 + 7 = 14$

(4) $5 + 5 = 10$

(5) $6 + 6 = 12$

(6) $4 + 4 = 8$

(7) $8 + 8 = 16$

(8) $9 + 9 = 18$

2 Add.

3 points per question

(1) $2 + 2 + 2 = 6$

(2) $3 + 3 + 3 = 9$

(3) $6 + 6 + 6 = 18$

(4) $7 + 7 + 7 = 21$

(5) $4 + 4 + 4 = 12$

(6) $8 + 8 + 8 = 24$

3 Add.

4 points per question

(1) $2 + 2 + 2 + 2 = 8$

(2) $5 + 5 + 5 + 5 = 20$

(3) $6 + 6 + 6 + 6 = 24$

(4) $4 + 4 + 4 + 4 = 16$

4 Add.

(1) $2 + 2 + 2 = 6$

(2) $2 + 2 + 2 + 2 = 8$

(3) $2 + 2 + 2 + 2 + 2 = 10$

(4) $2 + 2 + 2 + 2 + 2 + 2 = 12$

(5) $2 + 2 + 2 + 2 + 2 + 2 + 2 = 14$

(6) $2 + 2 + 2 + 2 + 2 + 2 + 2 + 2 = 16$

(7) $2 + 2 + 2 + 2 + 2 + 2 + 2 + 2 + 2 = 18$

(8) $3 + 3 + 3 = 9$

(9) $3 + 3 + 3 + 3 = 12$

(10) $3 + 3 + 3 + 3 + 3 = 15$

(11) $3 + 3 + 3 + 3 + 3 + 3 = 18$

(12) $3 + 3 + 3 + 3 + 3 + 3 + 3 = 21$

(13) $3 + 3 + 3 + 3 + 3 + 3 + 3 + 3 = 24$

(14) $3 + 3 + 3 + 3 + 3 + 3 + 3 + 3 + 3 = 24$

Do you see a pattern in the answers?

1 Add.

4 points per question

(1) $4 + 4 + 4 = 12$

(2) $4 + 4 + 4 + 4 = 16$

(3) $4 + 4 + 4 + 4 + 4 = 20$

(4) $4 + 4 + 4 + 4 + 4 + 4 = 24$

(5) $4 + 4 + 4 + 4 + 4 + 4 + 4 = 28$

(6) $4 + 4 + 4 + 4 + 4 + 4 + 4 + 4 = 32$

(7) $5 + 5 + 5 = 15$

(8) $5 + 5 + 5 + 5 = 20$

(9) $5 + 5 + 5 + 5 + 5 = 25$

(10) $5 + 5 + 5 + 5 + 5 + 5 = 30$

(11) $5 + 5 + 5 + 5 + 5 + 5 + 5 = 35$

(12) $5 + 5 + 5 + 5 + 5 + 5 + 5 + 5 = 40$

2 **Add.**

(1) $6+6+6=$ 18

(2) $6+6+6+6=$ 24

(3) $6+6+6+6+6=$ 30

(4) $6+6+6+6+6+6=$ 36

(5) $6+6+6+6+6+6+6=$ 42

(6) $6+6+6+6+6+6+6+6=$ 48

(7) $7+7+7=$ 22

(8) $7+7+7+7=$ 29

(9) $7+7+7+7+7=$ 36

(10) $7+7+7+7+7+7=$ 43

(11) $7+7+7+7+7+7+7=$ 50

(12) $7+7+7+7+7+7+7+7=$ 57

(13) $7+7+7+7+7+7+7+7+7=$ 64

Good job! How many times did you add the same number in each exercise?

5

Repeated Addition

Date I / D / C

Name

Level ☆

Score /100

1 Add.

4 points per question

(1) $8 + 8 + 8 = 24$

(2) $8 + 8 + 8 + 8 = 32$

(3) $8 + 8 + 8 + 8 + 8 = 40$

(4) $8 + 8 + 8 + 8 + 8 + 8 = 48$

(5) $8 + 8 + 8 + 8 + 8 + 8 + 8 = 56$

(6) $8 + 8 + 8 + 8 + 8 + 8 + 8 + 8 = 64$

(7) $9 + 9 + 9 = 27$

(8) $9 + 9 + 9 + 9 = 36$

(9) $9 + 9 + 9 + 9 + 9 = 45$

(10) $9 + 9 + 9 + 9 + 9 + 9 = 54$

(11) $9 + 9 + 9 + 9 + 9 + 9 + 9 = 63$

(12) $9 + 9 + 9 + 9 + 9 + 9 + 9 + 9 = 72$

2 Add.

(1) $1 + 1 + 1 =$

(2) $1 + 1 + 1 + 1 =$

(3) $1 + 1 + 1 + 1 + 1 =$

(4) $1 + 1 + 1 + 1 + 1 + 1 =$

(5) $1 + 1 + 1 + 1 + 1 + 1 + 1 =$

3 Add.

(1) $2 + 2 + 2 =$

(2) $3 + 3 + 3 + 3 + 3 =$

(3) $4 + 4 + 4 + 4 + 4 + 4 + 4 =$

(4) $5 + 5 + 5 + 5 =$

(5) $6 + 6 + 6 + 6 + 6 + 6 =$

(6) $7 + 7 + 7 + 7 + 7 + 7 + 7 + 7 + 7 =$

(7) $8 + 8 =$

(8) $9 + 9 + 9 + 9 + 9 + 9 + 9 + 9 =$

Don't forget to check your answers when you're done!

Review ◆Repeated Addition

Level

Date   /   /

Name

Score

/100

1 Add.

4 points per question

(1) $3+3+3=$

(2) $5+5+5+5=$

(3) $4+4+4+4=$

(4) $7+7+7+7+7=$

(5) $2+2+2+2+2=$

(6) $6+6+6=$

(7) $5+5+5+5+5+5+5=$

(8) $4+4+4=$

(9) $8+8+8+8+8=$

(10) $1+1+1+1+1+1=$

(11) $3+3+3+3+3=$

(12) $5+5+5+5+5=$

(13) $9+9+9+9+9+9=$

② Add.

4 points per question

(1) $8+8+8=$

(2) $5+5+5+5+5+5=$

(3) $3+3+3+3+3+3+3+3+3=$

(4) $2+2+2+2+2+2+2=$

(5) $6+6+6+6=$

(6) $4+4+4+4+4=$

(7) $7+7+7+7=$

(8) $3+3+3+3=$

(9) $8+8+8+8+8=$

(10) $9+9+9+9+9+9+9+9+9=$

(11) $7+7+7+7+7+7+7=$

(12) $6+6+6+6+6+6+6+6=$

Is your repeated addition perfect?
Are you ready for multiplication? Let's go!

9

Multiplication 2×

Date   /   /

Name

Score

/100

1 Fill in the missing numbers in the boxes below.

4 points per question

(1) 2 — 4 — 6 — 8 — ☐ — ☐ — ☐

(2) 4 — 6 — 8 — 10 — ☐ — ☐ — ☐

(3) 6 — 8 — 10 — 12 — ☐ — ☐ — ☐

(4) 8 — 10 — 12 — 14 — ☐ — ☐ — ☐

(5) 10 — 12 — 14 — 16 — ☐ — ☐ — ☐

2 Trace the numbers while reading each sentence below. Then read the times table on the right.

1 point per question

(1) $2 \times 1 = 2$
Two times one is two.

(2) $2 \times 2 = 4$
Two times two is four.

(3) $2 \times 3 = 6$
Two times three is six.

(4) $2 \times 4 = 8$
Two times four is eight.

(5) $2 \times 5 = 10$
Two times five is ten.

(6) $2 \times 6 = 12$
Two times six is twelve.

(7) $2 \times 7 = 14$
Two times seven is fourteen.

(8) $2 \times 8 = 16$
Two times eight is sixteen.

(9) $2 \times 9 = 18$
Two times nine is eighteen.

Let's memorize!

The 2× Table

$2 \times 1 = 2$ Two times one is two.

$2 \times 2 = 4$ Two times two is four.

$2 \times 3 = 6$ Two times three is six.

$2 \times 4 = 8$ Two times four is eight.

$2 \times 5 = 10$ Two times five is ten.

$2 \times 6 = 12$ Two times six is twelve.

$2 \times 7 = 14$ Two times seven is fourteen.

$2 \times 8 = 16$ Two times eight is sixteen.

$2 \times 9 = 18$ Two times nine is eighteen.

Let's keep trying to memorize the twos times table together!

③ Fill in the boxes while reading the number sentences below.

2 points per question

(1) $2 \times 1 = \boxed{}$
Two times one is two.

(2) $2 \times 2 = \boxed{}$
Two times two is four.

(3) $2 \times 3 = \boxed{}$
Two times three is six.

(4) $2 \times 4 = \boxed{}$
Two times four is eight.

(5) $2 \times 5 = \boxed{}$
Two times five is ten.

(6) $2 \times 6 = \boxed{}$
Two times six is twelve.

(7) $2 \times 7 = \boxed{}$
Two times seven is fourteen.

(8) $2 \times 8 = \boxed{}$
Two times eight is sixteen.

(9) $2 \times 9 = \boxed{}$
Two times nine is eighteen.

(10) $2 \times 3 = \boxed{}$
Two times three is six.

④ Multiply.

3 points per question

(1) $2 \times 1 =$

(2) $2 \times 2 =$

(3) $2 \times 3 =$

(4) $2 \times 4 =$

(5) $2 \times 5 =$

(6) $2 \times 6 =$

(7) $2 \times 7 =$

(8) $2 \times 8 =$

(9) $2 \times 9 =$

(10) $2 \times 3 =$

(11) $2 \times 5 =$

(12) $2 \times 7 =$

(13) $2 \times 9 =$

(14) $2 \times 2 =$

(15) $2 \times 4 =$

(16) $2 \times 6 =$

(17) $2 \times 8 =$

Good job practicing your twos times table!

11

6 Multiplication 2×

Level ☆☆

Date   /   /

Name

Score

/ 100

1 Fill in the boxes while reading the number sentences below.

1 point per question

(1) □ × □ = □
Two times one is two.

(2) □ × □ = □
Two times two is four.

(3) □ × □ = □
Two times three is six.

(4) □ × □ = □
Two times four is eight.

(5) □ × □ = □
Two times five is ten.

(6) □ × □ = □
Two times six is twelve.

(7) □ × □ = □
Two times seven is fourteen.

(8) □ × □ = □
Two times eight is sixteen.

(9) □ × □ = □
Two times nine is eighteen.

(10) □ × □ = □
Two times two is four.

2 Multiply.

2 points per question

(1) $2 \times 5 =$

(2) $2 \times 6 =$

(3) $2 \times 7 =$

(4) $2 \times 1 =$

(5) $2 \times 2 =$

(6) $2 \times 3 =$

(7) $2 \times 4 =$

(8) $2 \times 7 =$

(9) $2 \times 8 =$

(10) $2 \times 9 =$

(11) $2 \times 4 =$

(12) $2 \times 3 =$

(13) $2 \times 2 =$

(14) $2 \times 1 =$

(15) $2 \times 9 =$

(16) $2 \times 8 =$

(17) $2 \times 7 =$

(18) $2 \times 6 =$

(19) $2 \times 5 =$

(20) $2 \times 4 =$

3 Fill in the boxes while reading the number sentences below.

1 point per question

(1) ☐ × ☐ = ☐
Two times two is four.

(2) ☐ × ☐ = ☐
Two times six is twelve.

(3) ☐ × ☐ = ☐
Two times eight is sixteen.

(4) ☐ × ☐ = ☐
Two times one is two.

(5) ☐ × ☐ = ☐
Two times three is six.

(6) ☐ × ☐ = ☐
Two times five is ten.

(7) ☐ × ☐ = ☐
Two times nine is eighteen.

(8) ☐ × ☐ = ☐
Two times seven is fourteen.

(9) ☐ × ☐ = ☐
Two times four is eight.

(10) ☐ × ☐ = ☐
Two times six is twelve.

4 Multiply.

2 points per question

(1) $2 \times 2 =$

(2) $2 \times 4 =$

(3) $2 \times 6 =$

(4) $2 \times 8 =$

(5) $2 \times 1 =$

(6) $2 \times 3 =$

(7) $2 \times 5 =$

(8) $2 \times 7 =$

(9) $2 \times 9 =$

(10) $2 \times 8 =$

(11) $2 \times 6 =$

(12) $2 \times 4 =$

(13) $2 \times 2 =$

(14) $2 \times 9 =$

(15) $2 \times 7 =$

(16) $2 \times 5 =$

(17) $2 \times 3 =$

(18) $2 \times 1 =$

(19) $2 \times 9 =$

(20) $2 \times 8 =$

Great work. Let's keep going!

7 Multiplication 2×

Level ☆☆

Date   /   /

Name

Score

/100

---

1 Fill in the boxes while reading the number sentences below.

1 point per question

(1) ☐ × ☐ = ☐
Two times two is

(2) ☐ × ☐ = ☐
Two times eight is

(3) ☐ × ☐ = ☐
Two times seven is

(4) ☐ × ☐ = ☐
Two times three is

(5) ☐ × ☐ = ☐
Two times four is

(6) ☐ × ☐ = ☐
Two times one is

(7) ☐ × ☐ = ☐
Two times nine is

(8) ☐ × ☐ = ☐
Two times six is

(9) ☐ × ☐ = ☐
Two times five is

(10) ☐ × ☐ = ☐
Two times eight is

---

2 Multiply.

2 points per question

(1) $2 \times 3 =$

(2) $2 \times 4 =$

(3) $2 \times 5 =$

(4) $2 \times 1 =$

(5) $2 \times 2 =$

(6) $2 \times 7 =$

(7) $2 \times 8 =$

(8) $2 \times 9 =$

(9) $2 \times 7 =$

(10) $2 \times 5 =$

(11) $2 \times 3 =$

(12) $2 \times 8 =$

(13) $2 \times 6 =$

(14) $2 \times 4 =$

(15) $2 \times 3 =$

(16) $2 \times 2 =$

(17) $2 \times 1 =$

(18) $2 \times 0 = 0$
Two times zero is zero.

(19) $2 \times 2 =$

(20) $2 \times 4 =$

(18) Remember that any number times 0 equals 0.

3 Multiply.

2 points per question

(1) $2 \times 8 =$

(2) $2 \times 3 =$

(3) $2 \times 1 =$

(4) $2 \times 6 =$

(5) $2 \times 9 =$

(6) $2 \times 4 =$

(7) $2 \times 2 =$

(8) $2 \times 3 =$

(9) $2 \times 7 =$

(10) $2 \times 5 =$

(11) $2 \times 8 =$

(12) $2 \times 0 =$

(13) $2 \times 9 =$

(14) $2 \times 6 =$

(15) $2 \times 5 =$

(16) $2 \times 1 =$

(17) $2 \times 4 =$

(18) $2 \times 6 =$

(19) $2 \times 3 =$

(20) $2 \times 7 =$

4 Fill in the boxes below.

1 point per question

(1) $2 \times \boxed{} = 2$

(2) $2 \times \boxed{} = 4$

(3) $2 \times \boxed{} = 6$

(4) $2 \times \boxed{} = 8$

(5) $2 \times \boxed{} = 10$

(6) $2 \times \boxed{} = 12$

(7) $2 \times \boxed{} = 14$

(8) $2 \times \boxed{} = 16$

(9) $2 \times \boxed{} = 18$

(10) $2 \times \boxed{} = 6$

Try asking yourself, for example, "Two times what number equals two?"

Did you master your twos times table?

Level ☆☆

Score

/100

Date / /

Name

1 Fill in the missing numbers in the boxes below.

4 points per question

(1) 3 — 6 — 9 — 12 — □ — □ — □

(2) 6 — 9 — 12 — 15 — □ — □ — □

(3) 9 — 12 — 15 — 18 — □ — □ — □

(4) 12 — 15 — 18 — 21 — □ — □ — □

(5) 15 — 18 — 21 — 24 — □ — □ — □

2 Trace the numbers while reading each sentence below. Then read the times table on the right.

1 point per question

(1) 3 × 1 = 3
Three times one is three.

(2) 3 × 2 = 6
Three times two is six.

(3) 3 × 3 = 9
Three times three is nine.

(4) 3 × 4 = 12
Three times four is twelve.

(5) 3 × 5 = 15
Three times five is fifteen.

(6) 3 × 6 = 18
Three times six is eighteen.

(7) 3 × 7 = 21
Three times seven is twenty-one.

(8) 3 × 8 = 24
Three times eight is twenty-four.

(9) 3 × 9 = 27
Three times nine is twenty-seven.

Let's memorize!

The 3 × Table

3 × 1 = 3   Three times one is three.

3 × 2 = 6   Three times two is six.

3 × 3 = 9   Three times three is nine.

3 × 4 = 12   Three times four is twelve.

3 × 5 = 15   Three times five is fifteen.

3 × 6 = 18   Three times six is eighteen.

3 × 7 = 21   Three times seven is twenty-one.

3 × 8 = 24   Three times eight is twenty-four.

3 × 9 = 27   Three times nine is twenty-seven.

Let's keep trying to memorize the threes times table together!

3 **Fill in the boxes while reading the number sentences below.**

(1) $3 \times 1 = \boxed{}$
Three times one is three.

(2) $3 \times 2 = \boxed{}$
Three times two is six.

(3) $3 \times 3 = \boxed{}$
Three times three is nine.

(4) $3 \times 4 = \boxed{}$
Three times four is twelve.

(5) $3 \times 5 = \boxed{}$
Three times five is fifteen.

(6) $3 \times 6 = \boxed{}$
Three times six is eighteen.

(7) $3 \times 7 = \boxed{}$
Three times seven is twenty-one.

(8) $3 \times 8 = \boxed{}$
Three times eight is twenty-four.

(9) $3 \times 9 = \boxed{}$
Three times nine is twenty-seven.

(10) $3 \times 4 = \boxed{}$
Three times four is twelve.

4 **Multiply.**

3 points per question

(1) $3 \times 1 =$

(2) $3 \times 2 =$

(3) $3 \times 3 =$

(4) $3 \times 4 =$

(5) $3 \times 5 =$

(6) $3 \times 6 =$

(7) $3 \times 7 =$

(8) $3 \times 8 =$

(9) $3 \times 9 =$

(10) $3 \times 3 =$

(11) $3 \times 5 =$

(12) $3 \times 7 =$

(13) $3 \times 9 =$

(14) $3 \times 2 =$

(15) $3 \times 4 =$

(16) $3 \times 6 =$

(17) $3 \times 8 =$

Good job practicing your threes times table!

9 Multiplication 3×

Level ★★

Score

/100

Date / /

Name

---

1 Fill in the boxes while reading the number sentences below.

1 point per question

(1) ☐ × ☐ = ☐
Three times one is three.

(2) ☐ × ☐ = ☐
Three times two is six.

(3) ☐ × ☐ = ☐
Three times three is nine.

(4) ☐ × ☐ = ☐
Three times four is twelve.

(5) ☐ × ☐ = ☐
Three times five is fifteen.

(6) ☐ × ☐ = ☐
Three times six is eighteen.

(7) ☐ × ☐ = ☐
Three times seven is twenty-one.

(8) ☐ × ☐ = ☐
Three times eight is twenty-four.

(9) ☐ × ☐ = ☐
Three times nine is twenty-seven.

(10) ☐ × ☐ = ☐
Three times two is six.

---

2 Multiply.

2 points per question

(1) $3 \times 5 =$

(2) $3 \times 6 =$

(3) $3 \times 7 =$

(4) $3 \times 1 =$

(5) $3 \times 2 =$

(6) $3 \times 3 =$

(7) $3 \times 4 =$

(8) $3 \times 7 =$

(9) $3 \times 8 =$

(10) $3 \times 9 =$

(11) $3 \times 4 =$

(12) $3 \times 3 =$

(13) $3 \times 2 =$

(14) $3 \times 1 =$

(15) $3 \times 9 =$

(16) $3 \times 8 =$

(17) $3 \times 7 =$

(18) $3 \times 6 =$

(19) $3 \times 5 =$

(20) $3 \times 4 =$

18   © Kumon Publishing Co., Ltd.

3 Fill in the boxes while reading the number sentences below.

1 point per question

(1) $\square \times \square = \square$
Three times two is six.

(2) $\square \times \square = \square$
Three times six is eighteen.

(3) $\square \times \square = \square$
Three times eight is twenty-four.

(4) $\square \times \square = \square$
Three times one is three.

(5) $\square \times \square = \square$
Three times three is nine.

(6) $\square \times \square = \square$
Three times seven is twenty-one.

(7) $\square \times \square = \square$
Three times nine is twenty-seven.

(8) $\square \times \square = \square$
Three times five is fifteen.

(9) $\square \times \square = \square$
Three times four is twelve.

(10) $\square \times \square = \square$
Three times six is eighteen.

4 Multiply.

2 points per question

(1) $3 \times 2 =$

(2) $3 \times 4 =$

(3) $3 \times 6 =$

(4) $3 \times 8 =$

(5) $3 \times 1 =$

(6) $3 \times 3 =$

(7) $3 \times 5 =$

(8) $3 \times 7 =$

(9) $3 \times 9 =$

(10) $3 \times 8 =$

(11) $3 \times 6 =$

(12) $3 \times 4 =$

(13) $3 \times 2 =$

(14) $3 \times 9 =$

(15) $3 \times 7 =$

(16) $3 \times 5 =$

(17) $3 \times 3 =$

(18) $3 \times 1 =$

(19) $3 \times 9 =$

(20) $3 \times 8 =$

Are you getting the hang of it?
Let's keep going!

10 Multiplication 3×

Level ★★

Score
/ 100

Date / /

Name

---

1 Fill in the boxes while reading the number sentences below.

1 point per question

(1) ☐ × ☐ = ☐
Three times five is

(2) ☐ × ☐ = ☐
Three times three is

(3) ☐ × ☐ = ☐
Three times eight is

(4) ☐ × ☐ = ☐
Three times two is

(5) ☐ × ☐ = ☐
Three times nine is

(6) ☐ × ☐ = ☐
Three times seven is

(7) ☐ × ☐ = ☐
Three times six is

(8) ☐ × ☐ = ☐
Three times one is

(9) ☐ × ☐ = ☐
Three times four is

(10) ☐ × ☐ = ☐
Three times eight is

---

2 Multiply.

2 points per question

(1) $3 \times 3 =$

(2) $3 \times 4 =$

(3) $3 \times 5 =$

(4) $3 \times 1 =$

(5) $3 \times 2 =$

(6) $3 \times 7 =$

(7) $3 \times 8 =$

(8) $3 \times 9 =$

(9) $3 \times 7 =$

(10) $3 \times 5 =$

(11) $3 \times 3 =$

(12) $3 \times 8 =$

(13) $3 \times 6 =$

(14) $3 \times 4 =$

(15) $3 \times 3 =$

(16) $3 \times 2 =$

(17) $3 \times 1 =$

(18) $3 \times 0 = 0$
Three times zero is zero.

(19) $3 \times 2 =$

(20) $3 \times 4 =$

(18) Remember that any number times 0 equals 0.

3 Multiply.

2 points per question

(1) 3 × 8 =

(2) 3 × 3 =

(3) 3 × 1 =

(4) 3 × 6 =

(5) 3 × 9 =

(6) 3 × 4 =

(7) 3 × 2 =

(8) 3 × 3 =

(9) 3 × 7 =

(10) 3 × 5 =

(11) 3 × 8 =

(12) 3 × 0 =

(13) 3 × 9 =

(14) 3 × 6 =

(15) 3 × 5 =

(16) 3 × 1 =

(17) 3 × 4 =

(18) 3 × 6 =

(19) 3 × 3 =

(20) 3 × 7 =

4 Fill in the boxes below.

1 point per question

(1) 3 × ☐ = 3

(2) 3 × ☐ = 6

(3) 3 × ☐ = 9

(4) 3 × ☐ = 12

(5) 3 × ☐ = 15

(6) 3 × ☐ = 18

(7) 3 × ☐ = 21

(8) 3 × ☐ = 24

(9) 3 × ☐ = 27

(10) 3 × ☐ = 9

Try asking yourself, for example, "Three times what number equals three?"

Did you master your threes times table?

11 Review ◆Multiplication 2×, 3×

Level ★★

Date   /   /

Name

Score
/100

1 **Multiply.**

2 points per question

(1) $2 \times 4 =$

(2) $2 \times 5 =$

(3) $2 \times 6 =$

(4) $3 \times 6 =$

(5) $3 \times 7 =$

(6) $3 \times 8 =$

(7) $3 \times 9 =$

(8) $2 \times 9 =$

(9) $2 \times 8 =$

(10) $2 \times 7 =$

(11) $2 \times 6 =$

(12) $3 \times 3 =$

(13) $3 \times 2 =$

(14) $3 \times 1 =$

(15) $2 \times 1 =$

(16) $2 \times 2 =$

(17) $2 \times 3 =$

(18) $3 \times 6 =$

(19) $3 \times 5 =$

(20) $3 \times 4 =$

2 **Fill in the boxes below.**

1 point per question

(1) $2 \times \boxed{} = 6$

(2) $2 \times \boxed{} = 8$

(3) $2 \times \boxed{} = 10$

(4) $3 \times \boxed{} = 3$

(5) $3 \times \boxed{} = 6$

(6) $2 \times \boxed{} = 18$

(7) $2 \times \boxed{} = 16$

(8) $3 \times \boxed{} = 21$

(9) $3 \times \boxed{} = 18$

(10) $3 \times \boxed{} = 15$

③ Multiply.

(1) $3 \times 5 =$

(2) $2 \times 0 =$

(3) $2 \times 2 =$

(4) $3 \times 8 =$

(5) $2 \times 1 =$

(6) $3 \times 4 =$

(7) $3 \times 9 =$

(8) $2 \times 6 =$

(9) $3 \times 3 =$

(10) $3 \times 7 =$

(11) $2 \times 4 =$

(12) $3 \times 0 =$

(13) $2 \times 5 =$

(14) $2 \times 8 =$

(15) $3 \times 2 =$

(16) $2 \times 9 =$

(17) $3 \times 1 =$

(18) $2 \times 3 =$

(19) $2 \times 7 =$

(20) $3 \times 6 =$

④ Fill in the boxes below.

(1) $2 \times \boxed{} = 12$

(2) $3 \times \boxed{} = 9$

(3) $2 \times \boxed{} = 2$

(4) $3 \times \boxed{} = 24$

(5) $2 \times \boxed{} = 18$

(6) $3 \times \boxed{} = 0$

(7) $2 \times \boxed{} = 4$

(8) $3 \times \boxed{} = 27$

(9) $2 \times \boxed{} = 14$

(10) $3 \times \boxed{} = 12$

Do you remember your twos and threes times tables?

Multiplication 4×

Date   /   /

Name

Score   /100

---

1 Fill in the missing numbers in the boxes below.

4 points per question

(1) $\boxed{4} - \boxed{8} - \boxed{12} - \boxed{16} - \boxed{} - \boxed{} - \boxed{}$

(2) $\boxed{8} - \boxed{12} - \boxed{16} - \boxed{20} - \boxed{} - \boxed{} - \boxed{}$

(3) $\boxed{12} - \boxed{16} - \boxed{20} - \boxed{24} - \boxed{} - \boxed{} - \boxed{}$

(4) $\boxed{16} - \boxed{20} - \boxed{24} - \boxed{28} - \boxed{} - \boxed{} - \boxed{}$

(5) $\boxed{20} - \boxed{24} - \boxed{28} - \boxed{32} - \boxed{} - \boxed{} - \boxed{}$

---

2 Trace the numbers while reading each sentence below. Then read the times table on the right.

1 point per question

(1) $4 \times 1 = 4$
Four times one is four.

(2) $4 \times 2 = 8$
Four times two is eight.

(3) $4 \times 3 = 12$
Four times three is twelve.

(4) $4 \times 4 = 16$
Four times four is sixteen.

(5) $4 \times 5 = 20$
Four times five is twenty.

(6) $4 \times 6 = 24$
Four times six is twenty-four.

(7) $4 \times 7 = 28$
Four times seven is twenty-eight.

(8) $4 \times 8 = 32$
Four times eight is thirty-two.

(9) $4 \times 9 = 36$
Four times nine is thirty-six.

Let's memorize!

The 4× Table

$4 \times 1 = 4$ Four times one is four.

$4 \times 2 = 8$ Four times two is eight.

$4 \times 3 = 12$ Four times three is twelve.

$4 \times 4 = 16$ Four times four is sixteen.

$4 \times 5 = 20$ Four times five is twenty.

$4 \times 6 = 24$ Four times six is twenty-four.

$4 \times 7 = 28$ Four times seven is twenty-eight.

$4 \times 8 = 32$ Four times eight is thirty-two.

$4 \times 9 = 36$ Four times nine is thirty-six.

Let's keep trying to memorize the fours times table together!

---

3 Fill in the boxes while reading the number sentences below.

2 points per question

(1) $4 \times 1 = \boxed{}$
Four times one is four.

(2) $4 \times 2 = \boxed{}$
Four times two is eight.

(3) $4 \times 3 = \boxed{}$
Four times three is twelve.

(4) $4 \times 4 = \boxed{}$
Four times four is sixteen.

(5) $4 \times 5 = \boxed{}$
Four times five is twenty.

(6) $4 \times 6 = \boxed{}$
Four times six is twenty-four.

(7) $4 \times 7 = \boxed{}$
Four times seven is twenty-eight.

(8) $4 \times 8 = \boxed{}$
Four times eight is thirty-two.

(9) $4 \times 9 = \boxed{}$
Four times nine is thirty-six.

(10) $4 \times 4 = \boxed{}$
Four times four is sixteen.

4 Multiply.

3 points per question

(1) $4 \times 1 =$

(2) $4 \times 2 =$

(3) $4 \times 3 =$

(4) $4 \times 4 =$

(5) $4 \times 5 =$

(6) $4 \times 6 =$

(7) $4 \times 7 =$

(8) $4 \times 8 =$

(9) $4 \times 9 =$

(10) $4 \times 3 =$

(11) $4 \times 5 =$

(12) $4 \times 7 =$

(13) $4 \times 9 =$

(14) $4 \times 2 =$

(15) $4 \times 4 =$

(16) $4 \times 6 =$

(17) $4 \times 8 =$

Good job practicing your fours times table!

Date   /   /

Name

Level ★★

Score
/100

1 Fill in the boxes while reading the number sentences below.

1 point per question

(1) ☐ × ☐ = ☐
Four times one is four.

(2) ☐ × ☐ = ☐
Four times two is eight.

(3) ☐ × ☐ = ☐
Four times three is twelve.

(4) ☐ × ☐ = ☐
Four times four is sixteen.

(5) ☐ × ☐ = ☐
Four times five is twenty.

(6) ☐ × ☐ = ☐
Four times six is twenty-four.

(7) ☐ × ☐ = ☐
Four times seven is twenty-eight.

(8) ☐ × ☐ = ☐
Four times eight is thirty-two.

(9) ☐ × ☐ = ☐
Four times nine is thirty-six.

(10) ☐ × ☐ = ☐
Four times six is twenty-four.

2 Multiply.

2 points per question

(1) $4 \times 5 =$

(2) $4 \times 6 =$

(3) $4 \times 7 =$

(4) $4 \times 1 =$

(5) $4 \times 2 =$

(6) $4 \times 3 =$

(7) $4 \times 4 =$

(8) $4 \times 7 =$

(9) $4 \times 8 =$

(10) $4 \times 9 =$

(11) $4 \times 4 =$

(12) $4 \times 3 =$

(13) $4 \times 2 =$

(14) $4 \times 1 =$

(15) $4 \times 9 =$

(16) $4 \times 8 =$

(17) $4 \times 7 =$

(18) $4 \times 6 =$

(19) $4 \times 5 =$

(20) $4 \times 4 =$

3 **Fill in the boxes while reading the number sentences below.**

1 point per question

(1) ☐ × ☐ = ☐
Four times three is twelve.

(2) ☐ × ☐ = ☐
Four times six is twenty-four.

(3) ☐ × ☐ = ☐
Four times eight is thirty-two.

(4) ☐ × ☐ = ☐
Four times two is eight.

(5) ☐ × ☐ = ☐
Four times one is four.

(6) ☐ × ☐ = ☐
Four times nine is thirty-six.

(7) ☐ × ☐ = ☐
Four times four is sixteen.

(8) ☐ × ☐ = ☐
Four times seven is twenty-eight.

(9) ☐ × ☐ = ☐
Four times five is twenty.

(10) ☐ × ☐ = ☐
Four times six is twenty-four.

4 **Multiply.**

2 points per question

(1) $4 \times 2 =$

(2) $4 \times 4 =$

(3) $4 \times 6 =$

(4) $4 \times 8 =$

(5) $4 \times 1 =$

(6) $4 \times 3 =$

(7) $4 \times 5 =$

(8) $4 \times 7 =$

(9) $4 \times 9 =$

(10) $4 \times 8 =$

(11) $4 \times 6 =$

(12) $4 \times 4 =$

(13) $4 \times 2 =$

(14) $4 \times 9 =$

(15) $4 \times 7 =$

(16) $4 \times 5 =$

(17) $4 \times 3 =$

(18) $4 \times 1 =$

(19) $4 \times 4 =$

(20) $4 \times 8 =$

Well done! Don't forget to check your answers.

14

Multiplication 4×

Date   /   /

Name

Level ★★

Score
/100

1 Fill in the boxes while reading the number sentences below.

1 point per question

(1) ☐ × ☐ = ☐
Four times eight is

(2) ☐ × ☐ = ☐
Four times three is

(3) ☐ × ☐ = ☐
Four times four is

(4) ☐ × ☐ = ☐
Four times two is

(5) ☐ × ☐ = ☐
Four times nine is

(6) ☐ × ☐ = ☐
Four times seven is

(7) ☐ × ☐ = ☐
Four times six is

(8) ☐ × ☐ = ☐
Four times one is

(9) ☐ × ☐ = ☐
Four times four is

(10) ☐ × ☐ = ☐
Four times five is

2 Multiply.

2 points per question

(1) $4 \times 3 =$

(2) $4 \times 4 =$

(3) $4 \times 5 =$

(4) $4 \times 1 =$

(5) $4 \times 2 =$

(6) $4 \times 7 =$

(7) $4 \times 8 =$

(8) $4 \times 9 =$

(9) $4 \times 7 =$

(10) $4 \times 5 =$

(11) $4 \times 3 =$

(12) $4 \times 8 =$

(13) $4 \times 6 =$

(14) $4 \times 4 =$

(15) $4 \times 3 =$

(16) $4 \times 2 =$

(17) $4 \times 1 =$

(18) $4 \times 0 =$

(19) $4 \times 2 =$

(20) $4 \times 4 =$

Let's practice the fours times table some more!

3 Multiply.

2 points per question

(1) $4 \times 7 =$

(2) $4 \times 2 =$

(3) $4 \times 5 =$

(4) $4 \times 9 =$

(5) $4 \times 8 =$

(6) $4 \times 0 =$

(7) $4 \times 4 =$

(8) $4 \times 1 =$

(9) $4 \times 9 =$

(10) $4 \times 6 =$

(11) $4 \times 3 =$

(12) $4 \times 5 =$

(13) $4 \times 2 =$

(14) $4 \times 7 =$

(15) $4 \times 5 =$

(16) $4 \times 1 =$

(17) $4 \times 4 =$

(18) $4 \times 6 =$

(19) $4 \times 3 =$

(20) $4 \times 8 =$

4 Fill in the boxes below.

1 point per question

(1) $4 \times \boxed{} = 4$

(2) $4 \times \boxed{} = 8$

(3) $4 \times \boxed{} = 12$

(4) $4 \times \boxed{} = 16$

(5) $4 \times \boxed{} = 20$

(6) $4 \times \boxed{} = 24$

(7) $4 \times \boxed{} = 28$

(8) $4 \times \boxed{} = 32$

(9) $4 \times \boxed{} = 36$

(10) $4 \times \boxed{} = 24$

Try asking yourself, for example, "Four times what number equals four?"

Did you master your fours times table?

29

Multiplication 5×

Date   /   /

Name

Score   /100

1 Fill in the missing numbers in the boxes below.

4 points per question

(1) 5 — 10 — 15 — 20 — ☐ — ☐ — ☐

(2) 10 — 15 — 20 — 25 — ☐ — ☐ — ☐

(3) 15 — 20 — 25 — 30 — ☐ — ☐ — ☐

(4) 20 — 25 — 30 — 35 — ☐ — ☐ — ☐

(5) 25 — 30 — 35 — 40 — ☐ — ☐ — ☐

2 Trace the numbers while reading each sentence below. Then read the times table on the right.

1 point per question

(1) 5 × 1 = 5
Five times one is five.

(2) 5 × 2 = 10
Five times two is ten.

(3) 5 × 3 = 15
Five times three is fifteen.

(4) 5 × 4 = 20
Five times four is twenty.

(5) 5 × 5 = 25
Five times five is twenty-five.

(6) 5 × 6 = 30
Five times six is thirty.

(7) 5 × 7 = 35
Five times seven is thirty-five.

(8) 5 × 8 = 40
Five times eight is forty.

(9) 5 × 9 = 45
Five times nine is forty-five.

Let's memorize!

The 5 × Table

5 × 1 = 5   Five times one is five.

5 × 2 = 10   Five times two is ten.

5 × 3 = 15   Five times three is fifteen.

5 × 4 = 20   Five times four is twenty.

5 × 5 = 25   Five times five is twenty-five.

5 × 6 = 30   Five times six is thirty.

5 × 7 = 35   Five times seven is thirty-five.

5 × 8 = 40   Five times eight is forty.

5 × 9 = 45   Five times nine is forty-five.

Let's keep trying to memorize the fives times table together!

3 **Fill in the boxes while reading the number sentences below.**

2 points per question

(1) $5 \times 1 =$ ☐
Five times one is five.

(2) $5 \times 2 =$ ☐
Five times two is ten.

(3) $5 \times 3 =$ ☐
Five times three is fifteen.

(4) $5 \times 4 =$ ☐
Five times four is twenty.

(5) $5 \times 5 =$ ☐
Five times five is twenty-five.

(6) $5 \times 6 =$ ☐
Five times six is thirty.

(7) $5 \times 7 =$ ☐
Five times seven is thirty-five.

(8) $5 \times 8 =$ ☐
Five times eight is forty.

(9) $5 \times 9 =$ ☐
Five times nine is forty-five.

(10) $5 \times 3 =$ ☐
Five times three is fifteen.

4 **Multiply.**

3 points per question

(1) $5 \times 1 =$

(2) $5 \times 2 =$

(3) $5 \times 3 =$

(4) $5 \times 4 =$

(5) $5 \times 5 =$

(6) $5 \times 6 =$

(7) $5 \times 7 =$

(8) $5 \times 8 =$

(9) $5 \times 9 =$

(10) $5 \times 3 =$

(11) $5 \times 5 =$

(12) $5 \times 7 =$

(13) $5 \times 9 =$

(14) $5 \times 2 =$

(15) $5 \times 4 =$

(16) $5 \times 6 =$

(17) $5 \times 8 =$

Good job practicing your fives times table!

Multiplication 5×

Date   /   /

Name

Score
/100

---

1 Fill in the boxes while reading the number sentences below.

1 point per question

(1) ☐ × ☐ = ☐
Five times one is five.

(2) ☐ × ☐ = ☐
Five times two is ten.

(3) ☐ × ☐ = ☐
Five times three is fifteen.

(4) ☐ × ☐ = ☐
Five times four is twenty.

(5) ☐ × ☐ = ☐
Five times five is twenty-five.

(6) ☐ × ☐ = ☐
Five times six is thirty.

(7) ☐ × ☐ = ☐
Five times seven is thirty-five.

(8) ☐ × ☐ = ☐
Five times eight is forty.

(9) ☐ × ☐ = ☐
Five times nine is forty-five.

(10) ☐ × ☐ = ☐
Five times three is fifteen.

---

2 Multiply.

2 points per question

(1) $5 \times 5 =$

(2) $5 \times 6 =$

(3) $5 \times 7 =$

(4) $5 \times 1 =$

(5) $5 \times 2 =$

(6) $5 \times 3 =$

(7) $5 \times 4 =$

(8) $5 \times 7 =$

(9) $5 \times 8 =$

(10) $5 \times 9 =$

(11) $5 \times 4 =$

(12) $5 \times 3 =$

(13) $5 \times 2 =$

(14) $5 \times 1 =$

(15) $5 \times 9 =$

(16) $5 \times 8 =$

(17) $5 \times 7 =$

(18) $5 \times 6 =$

(19) $5 \times 5 =$

(20) $5 \times 4 =$

---

3 Fill in the boxes while reading the number sentences below.

1 point per question

(1) $\boxed{} \times \boxed{} = \boxed{}$
Five times two is ten.

(2) $\boxed{} \times \boxed{} = \boxed{}$
Five times six is thirty.

(3) $\boxed{} \times \boxed{} = \boxed{}$
Five times eight is forty.

(4) $\boxed{} \times \boxed{} = \boxed{}$
Five times one is five.

(5) $\boxed{} \times \boxed{} = \boxed{}$
Five times three is fifteen.

(6) $\boxed{} \times \boxed{} = \boxed{}$
Five times seven is thirty-five.

(7) $\boxed{} \times \boxed{} = \boxed{}$
Five times nine is forty-five.

(8) $\boxed{} \times \boxed{} = \boxed{}$
Five times five is twenty-five.

(9) $\boxed{} \times \boxed{} = \boxed{}$
Five times four is twenty.

(10) $\boxed{} \times \boxed{} = \boxed{}$
Five times six is thirty.

4 Multiply.

2 points per question

(1) $5 \times 2 =$

(2) $5 \times 4 =$

(3) $5 \times 6 =$

(4) $5 \times 8 =$

(5) $5 \times 1 =$

(6) $5 \times 3 =$

(7) $5 \times 5 =$

(8) $5 \times 7 =$

(9) $5 \times 9 =$

(10) $5 \times 8 =$

(11) $5 \times 6 =$

(12) $5 \times 4 =$

(13) $5 \times 2 =$

(14) $5 \times 9 =$

(15) $5 \times 7 =$

(16) $5 \times 5 =$

(17) $5 \times 3 =$

(18) $5 \times 1 =$

(19) $5 \times 4 =$

(20) $5 \times 8 =$

You're doing really well. Let's keep going!

Level ★★

Score

/100

Date / /

Name

---

1 Fill in the boxes while reading the number sentences below.

1 point per question

(1) ☐ × ☐ = ☐
Five times eight is

(2) ☐ × ☐ = ☐
Five times three is

(3) ☐ × ☐ = ☐
Five times four is

(4) ☐ × ☐ = ☐
Five times two is

(5) ☐ × ☐ = ☐
Five times nine is

(6) ☐ × ☐ = ☐
Five times seven is

(7) ☐ × ☐ = ☐
Five times six is

(8) ☐ × ☐ = ☐
Five times one is

(9) ☐ × ☐ = ☐
Five times four is

(10) ☐ × ☐ = ☐
Five times five is

---

2 Multiply.

2 points per question

(1) $5 \times 3 =$

(2) $5 \times 4 =$

(3) $5 \times 5 =$

(4) $5 \times 1 =$

(5) $5 \times 2 =$

(6) $5 \times 7 =$

(7) $5 \times 8 =$

(8) $5 \times 9 =$

(9) $5 \times 7 =$

(10) $5 \times 5 =$

(11) $5 \times 3 =$

(12) $5 \times 8 =$

(13) $5 \times 6 =$

(14) $5 \times 4 =$

(15) $5 \times 3 =$

(16) $5 \times 2 =$

(17) $5 \times 1 =$

(18) $5 \times 0 =$

(19) $5 \times 2 =$

(20) $5 \times 4 =$

Let's practice the fives times table some more!

3 Multiply.

(1) $5 \times 7 =$

(2) $5 \times 2 =$

(3) $5 \times 5 =$

(4) $5 \times 9 =$

(5) $5 \times 8 =$

(6) $5 \times 0 =$

(7) $5 \times 4 =$

(8) $5 \times 1 =$

(9) $5 \times 9 =$

(10) $5 \times 6 =$

(11) $5 \times 3 =$

(12) $5 \times 5 =$

(13) $5 \times 2 =$

(14) $5 \times 7 =$

(15) $5 \times 5 =$

(16) $5 \times 1 =$

(17) $5 \times 4 =$

(18) $5 \times 6 =$

(19) $5 \times 3 =$

(20) $5 \times 8 =$

4 Fill in the boxes below.

1 point per question

(1) $5 \times \boxed{} = 5$

(2) $5 \times \boxed{} = 10$

(3) $5 \times \boxed{} = 15$

(4) $5 \times \boxed{} = 20$

(5) $5 \times \boxed{} = 25$

(6) $5 \times \boxed{} = 30$

(7) $5 \times \boxed{} = 35$

(8) $5 \times \boxed{} = 40$

(9) $5 \times \boxed{} = 45$

(10) $5 \times \boxed{} = 15$

Try asking yourself, for example, "Five times what number equals five?"

Don't forget to check your answers when you're done.

Review ◆Multiplication 4×, 5×

Date / /

Name

Score / 100

1 Multiply.

2 points per question

(1) $4 \times 4 =$

(2) $4 \times 5 =$

(3) $4 \times 6 =$

(4) $5 \times 6 =$

(5) $5 \times 7 =$

(6) $5 \times 8 =$

(7) $5 \times 9 =$

(8) $4 \times 9 =$

(9) $4 \times 8 =$

(10) $4 \times 7 =$

(11) $4 \times 6 =$

(12) $5 \times 3 =$

(13) $5 \times 2 =$

(14) $5 \times 1 =$

(15) $4 \times 1 =$

(16) $4 \times 2 =$

(17) $4 \times 3 =$

(18) $5 \times 6 =$

(19) $5 \times 5 =$

(20) $5 \times 4 =$

2 Fill in the boxes below.

1 point per question

(1) $5 \times \boxed{} = 15$

(2) $5 \times \boxed{} = 20$

(3) $5 \times \boxed{} = 25$

(4) $4 \times \boxed{} = 4$

(5) $4 \times \boxed{} = 8$

(6) $5 \times \boxed{} = 45$

(7) $5 \times \boxed{} = 40$

(8) $4 \times \boxed{} = 28$

(9) $4 \times \boxed{} = 24$

(10) $4 \times \boxed{} = 20$

3 Multiply.

2 points per question

(1) $4 \times 5 =$

(2) $5 \times 0 =$

(3) $5 \times 2 =$

(4) $4 \times 8 =$

(5) $5 \times 1 =$

(6) $4 \times 4 =$

(7) $4 \times 9 =$

(8) $5 \times 6 =$

(9) $4 \times 3 =$

(10) $4 \times 7 =$

(11) $5 \times 4 =$

(12) $4 \times 0 =$

(13) $5 \times 5 =$

(14) $5 \times 8 =$

(15) $4 \times 2 =$

(16) $5 \times 9 =$

(17) $4 \times 1 =$

(18) $5 \times 3 =$

(19) $5 \times 7 =$

(20) $4 \times 6 =$

4 Fill in the boxes below.

1 point per question

(1) $5 \times \boxed{} = 30$

(2) $4 \times \boxed{} = 12$

(3) $5 \times \boxed{} = 5$

(4) $4 \times \boxed{} = 32$

(5) $5 \times \boxed{} = 45$

(6) $4 \times \boxed{} = 16$

(7) $5 \times \boxed{} = 10$

(8) $4 \times \boxed{} = 0$

(9) $5 \times \boxed{} = 35$

(10) $4 \times \boxed{} = 36$

Do you remember your fours and fives times tables?

19
Review ◆Multiplication 2× to 5×
Level

Date / /

Name

Score

/100

1 **Multiply.**

1 point per question

(1) $2 \times 2 =$

(2) $2 \times 4 =$

(3) $2 \times 6 =$

(4) $2 \times 5 =$

(5) $2 \times 7 =$

(6) $2 \times 9 =$

(7) $3 \times 3 =$

(8) $3 \times 5 =$

(9) $3 \times 7 =$

(10) $3 \times 4 =$

(11) $3 \times 6 =$

(12) $3 \times 8 =$

(13) $4 \times 2 =$

(14) $4 \times 4 =$

(15) $4 \times 6 =$

(16) $4 \times 8 =$

(17) $4 \times 5 =$

(18) $4 \times 7 =$

(19) $4 \times 9 =$

(20) $5 \times 8 =$

(21) $5 \times 6 =$

(22) $5 \times 4 =$

(23) $5 \times 9 =$

(24) $5 \times 7 =$

(25) $5 \times 5 =$

(26) $2 \times 3 =$

(27) $3 \times 4 =$

(28) $4 \times 5 =$

(29) $5 \times 1 =$

(30) $2 \times 8 =$

Let's practice the twos, threes, fours and fives times tables together!

2 Multiply.

2 points per question

(1) $2 \times 9 =$ (8) $5 \times 2 =$ (15) $2 \times 8 =$

(2) $3 \times 8 =$ (9) $3 \times 7 =$ (16) $4 \times 6 =$

(3) $4 \times 7 =$ (10) $5 \times 4 =$ (17) $5 \times 7 =$

(4) $5 \times 6 =$ (11) $2 \times 3 =$ (18) $4 \times 8 =$

(5) $2 \times 5 =$ (12) $4 \times 4 =$ (19) $3 \times 9 =$

(6) $3 \times 4 =$ (13) $3 \times 0 =$ (20) $2 \times 6 =$

(7) $4 \times 3 =$ (14) $5 \times 9 =$

3 Read each line from left to right. Then trace the correct values in this grid. Take the number on the side and multiply it by the number in the top row to get the correct value for each box.

15 points for completion

	2	3	4	5	6	7	8	9
2	4	6	8	10	12	14	16	18
3	6	9	12	15	18	21	24	27
4	8	12	16	20	24	28	32	36
5	10	15	20	25	30	35	40	45

4 Fill in the missing numbers to complete this grid. Take the number on the side and multiply it by the number in the top row to get the correct value for each box.

15 points for completion

	2	3	4	5	6	7	8	9
2	4	6		10	12		16	
3	6	9	12	15		21		27
4	8	12		20	24		32	
5	10	15	20		30	35		45

Did you remember your twos, threes, fours and fives times tables?

20

Level ★★

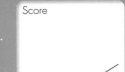

Date / /

Name

Score /100

1 **Fill in the missing numbers in the boxes below.**

4 points per question

(1) 6 — 12 — 18 — 24 — ☐ — ☐ — ☐

(2) 12 — 18 — 24 — 30 — ☐ — ☐ — ☐

(3) 18 — 24 — 30 — 36 — ☐ — ☐ — ☐

(4) 24 — 30 — 36 — 42 — ☐ — ☐ — ☐

(5) 30 — 36 — 42 — 48 — ☐ — ☐ — ☐

2 **Trace the numbers while reading each sentence below. Then read the times table on the right.**

1 point per question

(1) 6 × 1 = 6
Six times one is six.

(2) 6 × 2 = 12
Six times two is twelve.

(3) 6 × 3 = 18
Six times three is eighteen.

(4) 6 × 4 = 24
Six times four is twenty-four.

(5) 6 × 5 = 30
Six times five is thirty.

(6) 6 × 6 = 36
Six times six is thirty-six.

(7) 6 × 7 = 42
Six times seven is forty-two.

(8) 6 × 8 = 48
Six times eight is forty-eight.

(9) 6 × 9 = 54
Six times nine is fifty-four.

Let's memorize!

The 6 × Table

6 × 1 = 6   Six times one is six.

6 × 2 = 12   Six times two is twelve.

6 × 3 = 18   Six times three is eighteen.

6 × 4 = 24   Six times four is twenty-four.

6 × 5 = 30   Six times five is thirty.

6 × 6 = 36   Six times six is thirty-six.

6 × 7 = 42   Six times seven is forty-two.

6 × 8 = 48   Six times eight is forty-eight.

6 × 9 = 54   Six times nine is fifty-four.

Let's keep trying to memorize the sixes times table together!

3 Fill in the boxes while reading the number sentences below.

2 points per question

(1) $6 \times 1 =$ ☐
Six times one is six.

(2) $6 \times 2 =$ ☐
Six times two is twelve.

(3) $6 \times 3 =$ ☐
Six times three is eighteen.

(4) $6 \times 4 =$ ☐
Six times four is twenty-four.

(5) $6 \times 5 =$ ☐
Six times five is thirty.

(6) $6 \times 6 =$ ☐
Six times six is thirty-six.

(7) $6 \times 7 =$ ☐
Six times seven is forty-two.

(8) $6 \times 8 =$ ☐
Six times eight is forty-eight.

(9) $6 \times 9 =$ ☐
Six times nine is fifty-four.

(10) $6 \times 4 =$ ☐
Six times four is twenty-four.

4 Multiply.

3 points per question

(1) $6 \times 1 =$

(2) $6 \times 2 =$

(3) $6 \times 3 =$

(4) $6 \times 4 =$

(5) $6 \times 5 =$

(6) $6 \times 6 =$

(7) $6 \times 7 =$

(8) $6 \times 8 =$

(9) $6 \times 9 =$

(10) $6 \times 3 =$

(11) $6 \times 5 =$

(12) $6 \times 7 =$

(13) $6 \times 9 =$

(14) $6 \times 2 =$

(15) $6 \times 4 =$

(16) $6 \times 6 =$

(17) $6 \times 8 =$

Good job practicing your sixes times table!

Date / /

Name

Level ★★

Score /100

1 Fill in the boxes while reading the number sentences below.

1 point per question

(1) ☐ × ☐ = ☐
Six times one is six.

(2) ☐ × ☐ = ☐
Six times two is twelve.

(3) ☐ × ☐ = ☐
Six times three is eighteen.

(4) ☐ × ☐ = ☐
Six times four is twenty-four.

(5) ☐ × ☐ = ☐
Six times five is thirty.

(6) ☐ × ☐ = ☐
Six times six is thirty-six.

(7) ☐ × ☐ = ☐
Six times seven is forty-two.

(8) ☐ × ☐ = ☐
Six times eight is forty-eight.

(9) ☐ × ☐ = ☐
Six times nine is fifty-four.

(10) ☐ × ☐ = ☐
Six times six is thirty-six.

2 Multiply.

2 points per question

(1) $6 \times 5 =$

(2) $6 \times 6 =$

(3) $6 \times 7 =$

(4) $6 \times 1 =$

(5) $6 \times 2 =$

(6) $6 \times 3 =$

(7) $6 \times 4 =$

(8) $6 \times 7 =$

(9) $6 \times 8 =$

(10) $6 \times 9 =$

(11) $6 \times 4 =$

(12) $6 \times 3 =$

(13) $6 \times 2 =$

(14) $6 \times 1 =$

(15) $6 \times 9 =$

(16) $6 \times 8 =$

(17) $6 \times 7 =$

(18) $6 \times 6 =$

(19) $6 \times 5 =$

(20) $6 \times 4 =$

③ Fill in the boxes while reading the number sentences below.

1 point per question

(1) ☐ × ☐ = ☐
Six times three is eighteen.

(2) ☐ × ☐ = ☐
Six times six is thirty-six.

(3) ☐ × ☐ = ☐
Six times seven is forty-two.

(4) ☐ × ☐ = ☐
Six times one is six.

(5) ☐ × ☐ = ☐
Six times two is twelve.

(6) ☐ × ☐ = ☐
Six times eight is forty-eight.

(7) ☐ × ☐ = ☐
Six times nine is fifty-four.

(8) ☐ × ☐ = ☐
Six times five is thirty.

(9) ☐ × ☐ = ☐
Six times four is twenty-four.

(10) ☐ × ☐ = ☐
Six times three is eighteen.

④ Multiply.

2 points per question

(1) $6 \times 2 =$

(2) $6 \times 4 =$

(3) $6 \times 6 =$

(4) $6 \times 8 =$

(5) $6 \times 1 =$

(6) $6 \times 3 =$

(7) $6 \times 5 =$

(8) $6 \times 7 =$

(9) $6 \times 9 =$

(10) $6 \times 8 =$

(11) $6 \times 6 =$

(12) $6 \times 4 =$

(13) $6 \times 2 =$

(14) $6 \times 9 =$

(15) $6 \times 7 =$

(16) $6 \times 5 =$

(17) $6 \times 3 =$

(18) $6 \times 1 =$

(19) $6 \times 4 =$

(20) $6 \times 8 =$

You've made a lot of progress.
Keep up the good work!

Level ★★

Date / /

Name

Score

/100

1 Fill in the boxes while reading the number sentences below.

1 point per question

(1) ☐ × ☐ = ☐
Six times four is

(2) ☐ × ☐ = ☐
Six times eight is

(3) ☐ × ☐ = ☐
Six times six is

(4) ☐ × ☐ = ☐
Six times two is

(5) ☐ × ☐ = ☐
Six times three is

(6) ☐ × ☐ = ☐
Six times five is

(7) ☐ × ☐ = ☐
Six times nine is

(8) ☐ × ☐ = ☐
Six times seven is

(9) ☐ × ☐ = ☐
Six times one is

(10) ☐ × ☐ = ☐
Six times eight is

2 Multiply.

2 points per question

(1) $6 \times 3 =$

(2) $6 \times 4 =$

(3) $6 \times 5 =$

(4) $6 \times 1 =$

(5) $6 \times 2 =$

(6) $6 \times 7 =$

(7) $6 \times 8 =$

(8) $6 \times 9 =$

(9) $6 \times 7 =$

(10) $6 \times 5 =$

(11) $6 \times 3 =$

(12) $6 \times 8 =$

(13) $6 \times 6 =$

(14) $6 \times 4 =$

(15) $6 \times 3 =$

(16) $6 \times 2 =$

(17) $6 \times 1 =$

(18) $6 \times 0 =$

(19) $6 \times 2 =$

(20) $6 \times 4 =$

Let's practice the sixes times table some more!

3 Multiply.

2 points per question

(1) $6 \times 7 =$

(2) $6 \times 2 =$

(3) $6 \times 5 =$

(4) $6 \times 9 =$

(5) $6 \times 8 =$

(6) $6 \times 0 =$

(7) $6 \times 4 =$

(8) $6 \times 1 =$

(9) $6 \times 9 =$

(10) $6 \times 6 =$

(11) $6 \times 3 =$

(12) $6 \times 5 =$

(13) $6 \times 2 =$

(14) $6 \times 7 =$

(15) $6 \times 5 =$

(16) $6 \times 1 =$

(17) $6 \times 4 =$

(18) $6 \times 6 =$

(19) $6 \times 3 =$

(20) $6 \times 8 =$

4 Fill in the boxes below.

1 point per question

(1) $6 \times \boxed{} = 6$

(2) $6 \times \boxed{} = 12$

(3) $6 \times \boxed{} = 18$

(4) $6 \times \boxed{} = 24$

(5) $6 \times \boxed{} = 30$

(6) $6 \times \boxed{} = 36$

(7) $6 \times \boxed{} = 42$

(8) $6 \times \boxed{} = 48$

(9) $6 \times \boxed{} = 54$

(10) $6 \times \boxed{} = 18$

Did you master your sixes times table?

Multiplication 7×

Level

Score /100

1 **Fill in the missing numbers in the boxes below.**

4 points per question

(1) 7 — 14 — 21 — 28 — ☐ — ☐ — ☐

(2) 14 — 21 — 28 — 35 — ☐ — ☐ — ☐

(3) 21 — 28 — 35 — 42 — ☐ — ☐ — ☐

(4) 28 — 35 — 42 — 49 — ☐ — ☐ — ☐

(5) 35 — 42 — 49 — 56 — ☐ — ☐ — ☐

2 **Trace the numbers while reading each sentence below. Then read the times table on the right.**

1 point per question

(1) 7 × 1 = 7
Seven times one is seven.

(2) 7 × 2 = 14
Seven times two is fourteen.

(3) 7 × 3 = 21
Seven times three is twenty-one.

(4) 7 × 4 = 28
Seven times four is twenty-eight.

(5) 7 × 5 = 35
Seven times five is thirty-five.

(6) 7 × 6 = 42
Seven times six is forty-two.

(7) 7 × 7 = 49
Seven times seven is forty-nine.

(8) 7 × 8 = 56
Seven times eight is fifty-six.

(9) 7 × 9 = 63
Seven times nine is sixty-three.

Let's memorize!

The 7 × Table

7 × 1 = 7   Seven times one is seven.

7 × 2 = 14   Seven times two is fourteen.

7 × 3 = 21   Seven times three is twenty-one.

7 × 4 = 28   Seven times four is twenty-eight.

7 × 5 = 35   Seven times five is thirty-five.

7 × 6 = 42   Seven times six is forty-two.

7 × 7 = 49   Seven times seven is forty-nine.

7 × 8 = 56   Seven times eight is fifty-six.

7 × 9 = 63   Seven times nine is sixty-three.

Let's keep trying to memorize the sevens times table together!

3 **Fill in the boxes while reading the number sentences below.**

2 points per question

(1) $7 \times 1 = \boxed{}$
Seven times one is seven.

(2) $7 \times 2 = \boxed{}$
Seven times two is fourteen.

(3) $7 \times 3 = \boxed{}$
Seven times three is twenty-one.

(4) $7 \times 4 = \boxed{}$
Seven times four is twenty-eight.

(5) $7 \times 5 = \boxed{}$
Seven times five is thirty-five.

(6) $7 \times 6 = \boxed{}$
Seven times six is forty-two.

(7) $7 \times 7 = \boxed{}$
Seven times seven is forty-nine.

(8) $7 \times 8 = \boxed{}$
Seven times eight is fifty-six.

(9) $7 \times 9 = \boxed{}$
Seven times nine is sixty-three.

(10) $7 \times 4 = \boxed{}$
Seven times four is twenty-eight.

4 **Multiply.**

3 points per question

(1) $7 \times 1 =$

(2) $7 \times 2 =$

(3) $7 \times 3 =$

(4) $7 \times 4 =$

(5) $7 \times 5 =$

(6) $7 \times 6 =$

(7) $7 \times 7 =$

(8) $7 \times 8 =$

(9) $7 \times 9 =$

(10) $7 \times 3 =$

(11) $7 \times 5 =$

(12) $7 \times 7 =$

(13) $7 \times 9 =$

(14) $7 \times 2 =$

(15) $7 \times 4 =$

(16) $7 \times 6 =$

(17) $7 \times 8 =$

Good job practicing your sevens times table!

Date / /

Name

1 Fill in the boxes while reading the number sentences below.

1 point per question

(1) ☐ × ☐ = ☐
Seven times one is seven.

(2) ☐ × ☐ = ☐
Seven times two is fourteen.

(3) ☐ × ☐ = ☐
Seven times three is twenty-one.

(4) ☐ × ☐ = ☐
Seven times four is twenty-eight.

(5) ☐ × ☐ = ☐
Seven times five is thirty-five.

(6) ☐ × ☐ = ☐
Seven times six is forty-two.

(7) ☐ × ☐ = ☐
Seven times seven is forty-nine.

(8) ☐ × ☐ = ☐
Seven times eight is fifty-six.

(9) ☐ × ☐ = ☐
Seven times nine is sixty-three.

(10) ☐ × ☐ = ☐
Seven times four is twenty-eight.

2 Multiply.

2 points per question

(1) $7 \times 5 =$

(2) $7 \times 6 =$

(3) $7 \times 7 =$

(4) $7 \times 1 =$

(5) $7 \times 2 =$

(6) $7 \times 3 =$

(7) $7 \times 4 =$

(8) $7 \times 7 =$

(9) $7 \times 8 =$

(10) $7 \times 9 =$

(11) $7 \times 4 =$

(12) $7 \times 3 =$

(13) $7 \times 2 =$

(14) $7 \times 1 =$

(15) $7 \times 9 =$

(16) $7 \times 8 =$

(17) $7 \times 7 =$

(18) $7 \times 6 =$

(19) $7 \times 5 =$

(20) $7 \times 4 =$

3 **Fill in the boxes while reading the number sentences below.**

1 point per question

(1) □ × □ = □
Seven times two is fourteen.

(2) □ × □ = □
Seven times six is forty-two.

(3) □ × □ = □
Seven times eight is fifty-six.

(4) □ × □ = □
Seven times one is seven.

(5) □ × □ = □
Seven times three is twenty-one.

(6) □ × □ = □
Seven times seven is forty-nine.

(7) □ × □ = □
Seven times nine is sixty-three.

(8) □ × □ = □
Seven times five is thirty-five.

(9) □ × □ = □
Seven times four is twenty-eight.

(10) □ × □ = □
Seven times eight is fifty-six.

4 **Multiply.**

2 points per question

(1) $7 \times 2 =$

(2) $7 \times 4 =$

(3) $7 \times 6 =$

(4) $7 \times 8 =$

(5) $7 \times 1 =$

(6) $7 \times 3 =$

(7) $7 \times 5 =$

(8) $7 \times 7 =$

(9) $7 \times 9 =$

(10) $7 \times 8 =$

(11) $7 \times 6 =$

(12) $7 \times 4 =$

(13) $7 \times 2 =$

(14) $7 \times 9 =$

(15) $7 \times 7 =$

(16) $7 \times 5 =$

(17) $7 \times 3 =$

(18) $7 \times 1 =$

(19) $7 \times 4 =$

(20) $7 \times 8 =$

Don't forget to check your answers.

Multiplication 7×

Level ★★

Date / /

Name

Score /100

1 Fill in the boxes while reading the number sentences below.

1 point per question

(1) □ × □ = □
Seven times five is

(2) □ × □ = □
Seven times three is

(3) □ × □ = □
Seven times four is

(4) □ × □ = □
Seven times two is

(5) □ × □ = □
Seven times nine is

(6) □ × □ = □
Seven times seven is

(7) □ × □ = □
Seven times six is

(8) □ × □ = □
Seven times one is

(9) □ × □ = □
Seven times eight is

(10) □ × □ = □
Seven times five is

2 Multiply.

2 points per question

(1) $7 \times 3 =$

(2) $7 \times 4 =$

(3) $7 \times 5 =$

(4) $7 \times 1 =$

(5) $7 \times 2 =$

(6) $7 \times 7 =$

(7) $7 \times 8 =$

(8) $7 \times 9 =$

(9) $7 \times 7 =$

(10) $7 \times 5 =$

(11) $7 \times 3 =$

(12) $7 \times 8 =$

(13) $7 \times 6 =$

(14) $7 \times 4 =$

(15) $7 \times 3 =$

(16) $7 \times 2 =$

(17) $7 \times 1 =$

(18) $7 \times 0 =$

(19) $7 \times 2 =$

(20) $7 \times 4 =$

③ Multiply.

2 points per question

(1) 7 × 7 =

(2) 7 × 2 =

(3) 7 × 5 =

(4) 7 × 9 =

(5) 7 × 8 =

(6) 7 × 0 =

(7) 7 × 4 =

(8) 7 × 1 =

(9) 7 × 9 =

(10) 7 × 6 =

(11) 7 × 3 =

(12) 7 × 5 =

(13) 7 × 2 =

(14) 7 × 7 =

(15) 7 × 5 =

(16) 7 × 1 =

(17) 7 × 4 =

(18) 7 × 6 =

(19) 7 × 3 =

(20) 7 × 8 =

④ Fill in the boxes below.

1 point per question

(1) 7 × ☐ = 7

(2) 7 × ☐ = 14

(3) 7 × ☐ = 21

(4) 7 × ☐ = 28

(5) 7 × ☐ = 35

(6) 7 × ☐ = 42

(7) 7 × ☐ = 49

(8) 7 × ☐ = 56

(9) 7 × ☐ = 63

(10) 7 × ☐ = 28

Try asking yourself, for example, "Seven times what number equals seven?"

Did you master your sevens times table?

26

Review ◆Multiplication 6×, 7×

Level

Score

/100

Date   /   /

Name

1 Multiply.

2 points per question

(1) $6 \times 4 =$

(2) $6 \times 5 =$

(3) $6 \times 6 =$

(4) $7 \times 6 =$

(5) $7 \times 7 =$

(6) $7 \times 8 =$

(7) $7 \times 9 =$

(8) $6 \times 9 =$

(9) $6 \times 8 =$

(10) $6 \times 7 =$

(11) $6 \times 6 =$

(12) $7 \times 3 =$

(13) $7 \times 2 =$

(14) $7 \times 1 =$

(15) $6 \times 1 =$

(16) $6 \times 2 =$

(17) $6 \times 3 =$

(18) $7 \times 6 =$

(19) $7 \times 5 =$

(20) $7 \times 4 =$

2 Fill in the boxes below.

1 point per question

(1) $6 \times \boxed{} = 18$

(2) $6 \times \boxed{} = 24$

(3) $6 \times \boxed{} = 30$

(4) $7 \times \boxed{} = 7$

(5) $7 \times \boxed{} = 14$

(6) $6 \times \boxed{} = 54$

(7) $6 \times \boxed{} = 48$

(8) $7 \times \boxed{} = 49$

(9) $7 \times \boxed{} = 42$

(10) $7 \times \boxed{} = 35$

3 **Multiply.**

2 points per question

(1) $7 \times 5 =$

(2) $6 \times 0 =$

(3) $6 \times 2 =$

(4) $7 \times 8 =$

(5) $6 \times 1 =$

(6) $7 \times 4 =$

(7) $7 \times 9 =$

(8) $6 \times 6 =$

(9) $7 \times 3 =$

(10) $7 \times 7 =$

(11) $6 \times 4 =$

(12) $7 \times 0 =$

(13) $6 \times 5 =$

(14) $6 \times 8 =$

(15) $7 \times 2 =$

(16) $6 \times 9 =$

(17) $7 \times 1 =$

(18) $6 \times 3 =$

(19) $6 \times 7 =$

(20) $7 \times 6 =$

4 **Fill in the boxes below.**

1 point per question

(1) $6 \times \boxed{} = 36$

(2) $7 \times \boxed{} = 56$

(3) $6 \times \boxed{} = 6$

(4) $7 \times \boxed{} = 21$

(5) $6 \times \boxed{} = 54$

(6) $7 \times \boxed{} = 28$

(7) $6 \times \boxed{} = 12$

(8) $7 \times \boxed{} = 0$

(9) $6 \times \boxed{} = 42$

(10) $7 \times \boxed{} = 63$

Do you remember your sixes and sevens times tables?

1 Multiply.

1 point per question

(1) 2 × 9 =

(2) 2 × 7 =

(3) 2 × 5 =

(4) 2 × 3 =

(5) 3 × 8 =

(6) 3 × 6 =

(7) 3 × 4 =

(8) 3 × 2 =

(9) 4 × 8 =

(10) 4 × 6 =

(11) 4 × 4 =

(12) 4 × 2 =

(13) 5 × 9 =

(14) 5 × 7 =

(15) 5 × 5 =

(16) 5 × 3 =

(17) 6 × 2 =

(18) 6 × 4 =

(19) 6 × 6 =

(20) 6 × 8 =

(21) 7 × 1 =

(22) 7 × 3 =

(23) 7 × 5 =

(24) 7 × 7 =

(25) 7 × 9 =

(26) 2 × 8 =

(27) 3 × 3 =

(28) 4 × 9 =

(29) 5 × 2 =

(30) 6 × 1 =

(31) 7 × 8 =

(32) 2 × 6 =

(33) 4 × 7 =

(34) 6 × 3 =

(35) 3 × 5 =

(36) 5 × 4 =

(37) 7 × 6 =

(38) 2 × 4 =

(39) 5 × 8 =

(40) 3 × 7 =

(41) 6 × 5 =

(42) 2 × 2 =

(43) 3 × 9 =

(44) 5 × 6 =

(45) 7 × 4 =

2 Multiply.

1 point per question

(1) $2 \times 7 =$ (6) $7 \times 4 =$ (11) $5 \times 9 =$

(2) $3 \times 2 =$ (7) $2 \times 6 =$ (12) $7 \times 3 =$

(3) $4 \times 8 =$ (8) $4 \times 3 =$ (13) $2 \times 0 =$

(4) $5 \times 5 =$ (9) $6 \times 7 =$ (14) $5 \times 4 =$

(5) $6 \times 9 =$ (10) $3 \times 1 =$ (15) $3 \times 6 =$

3 Read each line from left to right. Then trace and write the correct values in this grid. Take the number on the side and multiply it by the number in the top row to get the correct value for each box.

20 points for completion

	2	3	4	5	6	7	8	9
2	4		8		12		16	
3		9		15		21		27
4	8		16		24		32	
5		15		25		35		45
6	12	18	24	30	36	42	48	54
7	14	21	28	35	42	49	56	63

4 Fill in the missing numbers to complete this grid. Take the number on the side and multiply it by the number in the top row to get the correct value for each box.

20 points for completion

	2	3	4	5	6	7	8	9
2		6		10		14		18
3	6		12		18		24	
4		12		20		28		36
5	10		20		30		40	
6		18		30		42		54
7	14		28		42		56	

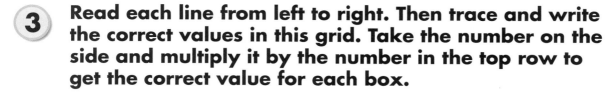

Did you remember your twos, threes, fours, fives, sixes and sevens times tables? Good job!

28

Level ★★

Date　　/　　/

Name

Score　　/100

1 Fill in the missing numbers in the boxes below.

4 points per question

(1)　8 — 16 — 24 — 32 — ☐ — ☐ — ☐

(2)　16 — 24 — 32 — 40 — ☐ — ☐ — ☐

(3)　24 — 32 — 40 — 48 — ☐ — ☐ — ☐

(4)　32 — 40 — 48 — 56 — ☐ — ☐ — ☐

(5)　40 — 48 — 56 — 64 — ☐ — ☐ — ☐

2 Trace the numbers while reading each sentence below. Then read the times table on the right.

1 point per question

(1)　$8 \times 1 = 8$
Eight times one is eight.

(2)　$8 \times 2 = 16$
Eight times two is sixteen.

(3)　$8 \times 3 = 24$
Eight times three is twenty-four.

(4)　$8 \times 4 = 32$
Eight times four is thirty-two.

(5)　$8 \times 5 = 40$
Eight times five is forty.

(6)　$8 \times 6 = 48$
Eight times six is forty-eight.

(7)　$8 \times 7 = 56$
Eight times seven is fifty-six.

(8)　$8 \times 8 = 64$
Eight times eight is sixty-four.

(9)　$8 \times 9 = 72$
Eight times nine is seventy-two.

Let's memorize!

The 8 × Table

$8 \times 1 = 8$　　Eight times one is eight.

$8 \times 2 = 16$　　Eight times two is sixteen.

$8 \times 3 = 24$　　Eight times three is twenty-four.

$8 \times 4 = 32$　　Eight times four is thirty-two.

$8 \times 5 = 40$　　Eight times five is forty.

$8 \times 6 = 48$　　Eight times six is forty-eight.

$8 \times 7 = 56$　　Eight times seven is fifty-six.

$8 \times 8 = 64$　　Eight times eight is sixty-four.

$8 \times 9 = 72$　　Eight times nine is seventy-two.

Let's keep trying to memorize the eights times table together!

　© Kumon Publishing Co., Ltd.

3 Fill in the boxes while reading the number sentences below.

2 points per question

(1) $8 \times 1 = \boxed{}$
Eight times one is eight.

(2) $8 \times 2 = \boxed{}$
Eight times two is sixteen.

(3) $8 \times 3 = \boxed{}$
Eight times three is twenty-four.

(4) $8 \times 4 = \boxed{}$
Eight times four is thirty-two.

(5) $8 \times 5 = \boxed{}$
Eight times five is forty.

(6) $8 \times 6 = \boxed{}$
Eight times six is forty-eight.

(7) $8 \times 7 = \boxed{}$
Eight times seven is fifty-six.

(8) $8 \times 8 = \boxed{}$
Eight times eight is sixty-four.

(9) $8 \times 9 = \boxed{}$
Eight times nine is seventy-two.

(10) $8 \times 4 = \boxed{}$
Eight times four is thirty-two.

4 Multiply.

3 points per question

(1) $8 \times 1 =$

(2) $8 \times 2 =$

(3) $8 \times 3 =$

(4) $8 \times 4 =$

(5) $8 \times 5 =$

(6) $8 \times 6 =$

(7) $8 \times 7 =$

(8) $8 \times 8 =$

(9) $8 \times 9 =$

(10) $8 \times 3 =$

(11) $8 \times 5 =$

(12) $8 \times 7 =$

(13) $8 \times 9 =$

(14) $8 \times 2 =$

(15) $8 \times 4 =$

(16) $8 \times 6 =$

(17) $8 \times 8 =$

Having fun practicing your eights times table?

1 Fill in the boxes while reading the number sentences below.

1 point per question

(1) ☐ × ☐ = ☐
Eight times one is eight.

(2) ☐ × ☐ = ☐
Eight times two is sixteen.

(3) ☐ × ☐ = ☐
Eight times three is twenty-four.

(4) ☐ × ☐ = ☐
Eight times four is thirty-two.

(5) ☐ × ☐ = ☐
Eight times five is forty.

(6) ☐ × ☐ = ☐
Eight times six is forty-eight.

(7) ☐ × ☐ = ☐
Eight times seven is fifty-six.

(8) ☐ × ☐ = ☐
Eight times eight is sixty-four.

(9) ☐ × ☐ = ☐
Eight times nine is seventy-two.

(10) ☐ × ☐ = ☐
Eight times four is thirty-two.

2 Multiply.

2 points per question

(1) $8 \times 5 =$

(2) $8 \times 6 =$

(3) $8 \times 7 =$

(4) $8 \times 1 =$

(5) $8 \times 2 =$

(6) $8 \times 3 =$

(7) $8 \times 4 =$

(8) $8 \times 7 =$

(9) $8 \times 8 =$

(10) $8 \times 9 =$

(11) $8 \times 4 =$

(12) $8 \times 3 =$

(13) $8 \times 2 =$

(14) $8 \times 1 =$

(15) $8 \times 9 =$

(16) $8 \times 8 =$

(17) $8 \times 7 =$

(18) $8 \times 6 =$

(19) $8 \times 5 =$

(20) $8 \times 4 =$

3 Fill in the boxes while reading the number sentences below.

1 point per question

(1) ☐ × ☐ = ☐
Eight times three is twenty-four.

(2) ☐ × ☐ = ☐
Eight times six is forty-eight.

(3) ☐ × ☐ = ☐
Eight times eight is sixty-four.

(4) ☐ × ☐ = ☐
Eight times two is sixteen.

(5) ☐ × ☐ = ☐
Eight times one is eight.

(6) ☐ × ☐ = ☐
Eight times seven is fifty-six.

(7) ☐ × ☐ = ☐
Eight times five is forty.

(8) ☐ × ☐ = ☐
Eight times four is thirty-two.

(9) ☐ × ☐ = ☐
Eight times nine is seventy-two.

(10) ☐ × ☐ = ☐
Eight times eight is sixty-four.

4 Multiply.

2 points per question

(1) $8 \times 2 =$

(2) $8 \times 4 =$

(3) $8 \times 6 =$

(4) $8 \times 8 =$

(5) $8 \times 1 =$

(6) $8 \times 3 =$

(7) $8 \times 5 =$

(8) $8 \times 7 =$

(9) $8 \times 9 =$

(10) $8 \times 8 =$

(11) $8 \times 6 =$

(12) $8 \times 4 =$

(13) $8 \times 2 =$

(14) $8 \times 9 =$

(15) $8 \times 7 =$

(16) $8 \times 5 =$

(17) $8 \times 3 =$

(18) $8 \times 1 =$

(19) $8 \times 4 =$

(20) $8 \times 8 =$

Good job practicing your eights times table!

Multiplication 8×

30

Level ★★

Score

Date   /   /

Name

/100

1 Fill in the boxes while reading the number sentences below.

1 point per question

(1) ☐ × ☐ = ☐
Eight times three is

(2) ☐ × ☐ = ☐
Eight times six is

(3) ☐ × ☐ = ☐
Eight times five is

(4) ☐ × ☐ = ☐
Eight times two is

(5) ☐ × ☐ = ☐
Eight times one is

(6) ☐ × ☐ = ☐
Eight times seven is

(7) ☐ × ☐ = ☐
Eight times nine is

(8) ☐ × ☐ = ☐
Eight times eight is

(9) ☐ × ☐ = ☐
Eight times four is

(10) ☐ × ☐ = ☐
Eight times three is

2 Multiply.

2 points per question

(1) $8 \times 3 =$

(2) $8 \times 4 =$

(3) $8 \times 5 =$

(4) $8 \times 1 =$

(5) $8 \times 2 =$

(6) $8 \times 7 =$

(7) $8 \times 8 =$

(8) $8 \times 9 =$

(9) $8 \times 7 =$

(10) $8 \times 5 =$

(11) $8 \times 3 =$

(12) $8 \times 8 =$

(13) $8 \times 6 =$

(14) $8 \times 4 =$

(15) $8 \times 3 =$

(16) $8 \times 2 =$

(17) $8 \times 1 =$

(18) $8 \times 0 =$

(19) $8 \times 2 =$

(20) $8 \times 4 =$

3 **Multiply.**

2 points per question

(1) $8 \times 7 =$

(2) $8 \times 2 =$

(3) $8 \times 5 =$

(4) $8 \times 9 =$

(5) $8 \times 8 =$

(6) $8 \times 0 =$

(7) $8 \times 4 =$

(8) $8 \times 1 =$

(9) $8 \times 9 =$

(10) $8 \times 6 =$

(11) $8 \times 3 =$

(12) $8 \times 5 =$

(13) $8 \times 2 =$

(14) $8 \times 7 =$

(15) $8 \times 5 =$

(16) $8 \times 1 =$

(17) $8 \times 4 =$

(18) $8 \times 6 =$

(19) $8 \times 3 =$

(20) $8 \times 8 =$

4 **Fill in the boxes below.**

1 point per question

(1) $8 \times \boxed{} = 8$

(2) $8 \times \boxed{} = 16$

(3) $8 \times \boxed{} = 24$

(4) $8 \times \boxed{} = 32$

(5) $8 \times \boxed{} = 40$

(6) $8 \times \boxed{} = 48$

(7) $8 \times \boxed{} = 56$

(8) $8 \times \boxed{} = 64$

(9) $8 \times \boxed{} = 72$

(10) $8 \times \boxed{} = 32$

Try asking yourself, for example, "Eight times what number equals eight?"

Did you master your eights times table?

Date   /   /

Name

1 **Fill in the missing numbers in the boxes below.**

4 points per question

(1) 9 — 18 — 27 — 36 — ☐ — ☐ — ☐

(2) 18 — 27 — 36 — 45 — ☐ — ☐ — ☐

(3) 27 — 36 — 45 — 54 — ☐ — ☐ — ☐

(4) 36 — 45 — 54 — 63 — ☐ — ☐ — ☐

(5) 45 — 54 — 63 — 72 — ☐ — ☐ — ☐

2 **Trace the numbers while reading each sentence below. Then read the times table on the right.**

1 point per question

(1) 9 × 1 = 9
Nine times one is nine.

(2) 9 × 2 = 18
Nine times two is eighteen.

(3) 9 × 3 = 27
Nine times three is twenty-seven.

(4) 9 × 4 = 36
Nine times four is thirty-six.

(5) 9 × 5 = 45
Nine times five is forty-five.

(6) 9 × 6 = 54
Nine times six is fifty-four.

(7) 9 × 7 = 63
Nine times seven is sixty-three.

(8) 9 × 8 = 72
Nine times eight is seventy-two.

(9) 9 × 9 = 81
Nine times nine is eighty-one.

Let's memorize!

The 9 × Table

9 × 1 = 9   Nine times one is nine.

9 × 2 = 18   Nine times two is eighteen.

9 × 3 = 27   Nine times three is twenty-seven.

9 × 4 = 36   Nine times four is thirty-six.

9 × 5 = 45   Nine times five is forty-five.

9 × 6 = 54   Nine times six is fifty-four.

9 × 7 = 63   Nine times seven is sixty-three.

9 × 8 = 72   Nine times eight is seventy-two.

9 × 9 = 81   Nine times nine is eighty-one.

Let's practice the nines times table!

3 **Fill in the boxes while reading the number sentences below.**

2 points per question

(1) $9 \times 1 = \boxed{}$
Nine times one is nine.

(2) $9 \times 2 = \boxed{}$
Nine times two is eighteen.

(3) $9 \times 3 = \boxed{}$
Nine times three is twenty-seven.

(4) $9 \times 4 = \boxed{}$
Nine times four is thirty-six.

(5) $9 \times 5 = \boxed{}$
Nine times five is forty-five.

(6) $9 \times 6 = \boxed{}$
Nine times six is fifty-four.

(7) $9 \times 7 = \boxed{}$
Nine times seven is sixty-three.

(8) $9 \times 8 = \boxed{}$
Nine times eight is seventy-two.

(9) $9 \times 9 = \boxed{}$
Nine times nine is eighty-one.

(10) $9 \times 4 = \boxed{}$
Nine times four is thirty-six.

4 **Multiply.**

3 points per question

(1) $9 \times 1 =$

(2) $9 \times 2 =$

(3) $9 \times 3 =$

(4) $9 \times 4 =$

(5) $9 \times 5 =$

(6) $9 \times 6 =$

(7) $9 \times 7 =$

(8) $9 \times 8 =$

(9) $9 \times 9 =$

(10) $9 \times 3 =$

(11) $9 \times 5 =$

(12) $9 \times 7 =$

(13) $9 \times 9 =$

(14) $9 \times 2 =$

(15) $9 \times 4 =$

(16) $9 \times 6 =$

(17) $9 \times 8 =$

Having fun practicing your nines times table?

32 Multiplication 9×

Date / /

Name

Score /100

1 Fill in the boxes while reading the number sentences below.

1 point per question

(1) ☐ × ☐ = ☐
Nine times one is nine.

(2) ☐ × ☐ = ☐
Nine times two is eighteen.

(3) ☐ × ☐ = ☐
Nine times three is twenty-seven.

(4) ☐ × ☐ = ☐
Nine times four is thirty-six.

(5) ☐ × ☐ = ☐
Nine times five is forty-five.

(6) ☐ × ☐ = ☐
Nine times six is fifty-four.

(7) ☐ × ☐ = ☐
Nine times seven is sixty-three.

(8) ☐ × ☐ = ☐
Nine times eight is seventy-two.

(9) ☐ × ☐ = ☐
Nine times nine is eighty-one.

(10) ☐ × ☐ = ☐
Nine times six is fifty-four.

2 Multiply.

2 points per question

(1) $9 \times 5 =$

(2) $9 \times 6 =$

(3) $9 \times 7 =$

(4) $9 \times 1 =$

(5) $9 \times 2 =$

(6) $9 \times 3 =$

(7) $9 \times 4 =$

(8) $9 \times 7 =$

(9) $9 \times 8 =$

(10) $9 \times 9 =$

(11) $9 \times 4 =$

(12) $9 \times 3 =$

(13) $9 \times 2 =$

(14) $9 \times 1 =$

(15) $9 \times 9 =$

(16) $9 \times 8 =$

(17) $9 \times 7 =$

(18) $9 \times 6 =$

(19) $9 \times 5 =$

(20) $9 \times 4 =$

3 **Fill in the boxes while reading the number sentences below.**

1 point per question

(1) ☐ × ☐ = ☐
Nine times two is eighteen.

(2) ☐ × ☐ = ☐
Nine times six is fifty-four.

(3) ☐ × ☐ = ☐
Nine times three is twenty-seven.

(4) ☐ × ☐ = ☐
Nine times seven is sixty-three.

(5) ☐ × ☐ = ☐
Nine times nine is eighty-one.

(6) ☐ × ☐ = ☐
Nine times one is nine.

(7) ☐ × ☐ = ☐
Nine times eight is seventy-two.

(8) ☐ × ☐ = ☐
Nine times five is forty-five.

(9) ☐ × ☐ = ☐
Nine times four is thirty-six.

(10) ☐ × ☐ = ☐
Nine times three is twenty-seven.

4 **Multiply.**

2 points per question

(1) $9 \times 2 =$

(2) $9 \times 4 =$

(3) $9 \times 6 =$

(4) $9 \times 8 =$

(5) $9 \times 1 =$

(6) $9 \times 3 =$

(7) $9 \times 5 =$

(8) $9 \times 7 =$

(9) $9 \times 9 =$

(10) $9 \times 8 =$

(11) $9 \times 6 =$

(12) $9 \times 4 =$

(13) $9 \times 2 =$

(14) $9 \times 9 =$

(15) $9 \times 7 =$

(16) $9 \times 5 =$

(17) $9 \times 3 =$

(18) $9 \times 1 =$

(19) $9 \times 4 =$

(20) $9 \times 6 =$

Good job! Don't forget to check your answers.

1 Fill in the boxes while reading the number sentences below.

1 point per question

(1) ☐ × ☐ = ☐
Nine times three is

(2) ☐ × ☐ = ☐
Nine times five is

(3) ☐ × ☐ = ☐
Nine times six is

(4) ☐ × ☐ = ☐
Nine times two is

(5) ☐ × ☐ = ☐
Nine times four is

(6) ☐ × ☐ = ☐
Nine times eight is

(7) ☐ × ☐ = ☐
Nine times nine is

(8) ☐ × ☐ = ☐
Nine times seven is

(9) ☐ × ☐ = ☐
Nine times one is

(10) ☐ × ☐ = ☐
Nine times five is

2 Multiply.

2 points per question

(1) $9 \times 3 =$

(2) $9 \times 4 =$

(3) $9 \times 5 =$

(4) $9 \times 1 =$

(5) $9 \times 2 =$

(6) $9 \times 7 =$

(7) $9 \times 8 =$

(8) $9 \times 9 =$

(9) $9 \times 7 =$

(10) $9 \times 5 =$

(11) $9 \times 3 =$

(12) $9 \times 8 =$

(13) $9 \times 6 =$

(14) $9 \times 4 =$

(15) $9 \times 3 =$

(16) $9 \times 2 =$

(17) $9 \times 1 =$

(18) $9 \times 0 =$

(19) $9 \times 2 =$

(20) $9 \times 4 =$

3 Multiply.

2 points per question

(1) $9 \times 7 =$

(2) $9 \times 2 =$

(3) $9 \times 5 =$

(4) $9 \times 9 =$

(5) $9 \times 8 =$

(6) $9 \times 0 =$

(7) $9 \times 4 =$

(8) $9 \times 1 =$

(9) $9 \times 9 =$

(10) $9 \times 6 =$

(11) $9 \times 3 =$

(12) $9 \times 5 =$

(13) $9 \times 2 =$

(14) $9 \times 7 =$

(15) $9 \times 5 =$

(16) $9 \times 1 =$

(17) $9 \times 4 =$

(18) $9 \times 6 =$

(19) $9 \times 3 =$

(20) $9 \times 8 =$

4 Fill in the boxes below.

1 point per question

(1) $9 \times \boxed{} = 9$

(2) $9 \times \boxed{} = 18$

(3) $9 \times \boxed{} = 27$

(4) $9 \times \boxed{} = 36$

(5) $9 \times \boxed{} = 45$

(6) $9 \times \boxed{} = 54$

(7) $9 \times \boxed{} = 63$

(8) $9 \times \boxed{} = 72$

(9) $9 \times \boxed{} = 81$

(10) $9 \times \boxed{} = 18$

Try asking yourself, for example, "Nine times what number equals nine?"

Did you master your nines times table?

1 Multiply.

2 points per question

(1) $8 \times 4 =$

(2) $8 \times 5 =$

(3) $8 \times 6 =$

(4) $9 \times 6 =$

(5) $9 \times 7 =$

(6) $9 \times 8 =$

(7) $9 \times 9 =$

(8) $8 \times 9 =$

(9) $8 \times 8 =$

(10) $8 \times 7 =$

(11) $8 \times 6 =$

(12) $9 \times 3 =$

(13) $9 \times 2 =$

(14) $9 \times 1 =$

(15) $8 \times 1 =$

(16) $8 \times 2 =$

(17) $8 \times 3 =$

(18) $9 \times 6 =$

(19) $9 \times 5 =$

(20) $9 \times 4 =$

2 Fill in the boxes below.

1 point per question

(1) $8 \times \boxed{} = 8$

(2) $8 \times \boxed{} = 16$

(3) $8 \times \boxed{} = 40$

(4) $9 \times \boxed{} = 36$

(5) $9 \times \boxed{} = 27$

(6) $8 \times \boxed{} = 56$

(7) $8 \times \boxed{} = 48$

(8) $9 \times \boxed{} = 81$

(9) $9 \times \boxed{} = 45$

(10) $9 \times \boxed{} = 72$

3 Multiply.

2 points per question

(1) $9 \times 5 =$

(2) $8 \times 0 =$

(3) $8 \times 2 =$

(4) $9 \times 8 =$

(5) $8 \times 1 =$

(6) $9 \times 4 =$

(7) $9 \times 9 =$

(8) $8 \times 6 =$

(9) $9 \times 3 =$

(10) $9 \times 7 =$

(11) $8 \times 4 =$

(12) $9 \times 0 =$

(13) $8 \times 5 =$

(14) $8 \times 8 =$

(15) $9 \times 2 =$

(16) $8 \times 9 =$

(17) $9 \times 1 =$

(18) $8 \times 3 =$

(19) $8 \times 7 =$

(20) $9 \times 6 =$

4 Fill in the boxes below.

1 point per question

(1) $9 \times \boxed{} = 54$

(2) $8 \times \boxed{} = 24$

(3) $9 \times \boxed{} = 81$

(4) $8 \times \boxed{} = 64$

(5) $9 \times \boxed{} = 9$

(6) $8 \times \boxed{} = 32$

(7) $9 \times \boxed{} = 63$

(8) $8 \times \boxed{} = 0$

(9) $9 \times \boxed{} = 18$

(10) $8 \times \boxed{} = 72$

Do you remember your eights and nines times tables?

Review ◆Multiplication 2× to 9×

35

Level ★★

Date / /

Name

Score

/100

1 Multiply.

1 point per question

(1) $2 \times 3 =$

(2) $2 \times 7 =$

(3) $3 \times 4 =$

(4) $3 \times 9 =$

(5) $4 \times 3 =$

(6) $4 \times 5 =$

(7) $4 \times 7 =$

(8) $5 \times 4 =$

(9) $5 \times 6 =$

(10) $5 \times 8 =$

(11) $6 \times 3 =$

(12) $6 \times 5 =$

(13) $6 \times 7 =$

(14) $7 \times 2 =$

(15) $7 \times 4 =$

(16) $7 \times 6 =$

(17) $7 \times 8 =$

(18) $8 \times 3 =$

(19) $8 \times 5 =$

(20) $8 \times 7 =$

(21) $8 \times 9 =$

(22) $9 \times 2 =$

(23) $9 \times 4 =$

(24) $9 \times 6 =$

(25) $9 \times 8 =$

(26) $2 \times 4 =$

(27) $2 \times 8 =$

(28) $3 \times 3 =$

(29) $3 \times 7 =$

(30) $4 \times 8 =$

(31) $4 \times 6 =$

(32) $4 \times 4 =$

(33) $5 \times 9 =$

(34) $5 \times 7 =$

(35) $5 \times 5 =$

(36) $6 \times 4 =$

(37) $6 \times 6 =$

(38) $6 \times 8 =$

(39) $7 \times 3 =$

(40) $7 \times 5 =$

2 Multiply.

2 points per question

(1) $2 \times 5 =$

(2) $3 \times 2 =$

(3) $4 \times 8 =$

(4) $5 \times 3 =$

(5) $6 \times 9 =$

(6) $7 \times 7 =$

(7) $8 \times 2 =$

(8) $9 \times 6 =$

(9) $3 \times 6 =$

(10) $5 \times 1 =$

(11) $7 \times 9 =$

(12) $9 \times 5 =$

(13) $2 \times 1 =$

(14) $4 \times 1 =$

(15) $6 \times 2 =$

(16) $8 \times 4 =$

(17) $6 \times 4 =$

(18) $3 \times 8 =$

(19) $8 \times 6 =$

(20) $4 \times 2 =$

(21) $7 \times 3 =$

(22) $2 \times 2 =$

(23) $9 \times 9 =$

(24) $5 \times 2 =$

(25) $8 \times 8 =$

(26) $2 \times 9 =$

(27) $6 \times 1 =$

(28) $3 \times 5 =$

(29) $9 \times 3 =$

(30) $2 \times 6 =$

Did you remember your twos, threes, fours, fives, sixes, sevens, eights and nines times tables? Good job!

36 Review ◆Multiplication 2× to 9×

Level

Date / /

Name

Score

/ 100

1 Multiply.

1 point per question

(1) 2 × 3 =

(2) 4 × 8 =

(3) 6 × 9 =

(4) 8 × 5 =

(5) 3 × 2 =

(6) 5 × 7 =

(7) 7 × 6 =

(8) 9 × 4 =

(9) 7 × 3 =

(10) 8 × 2 =

(11) 9 × 7 =

(12) 4 × 3 =

(13) 5 × 4 =

(14) 6 × 6 =

(15) 2 × 8 =

(16) 3 × 5 =

(17) 3 × 8 =

(18) 8 × 3 =

(19) 9 × 6 =

(20) 5 × 9 =

(21) 2 × 4 =

(22) 7 × 9 =

(23) 4 × 2 =

(24) 6 × 7 =

(25) 9 × 5 =

(26) 3 × 7 =

(27) 4 × 5 =

(28) 5 × 1 =

(29) 8 × 4 =

(30) 9 × 2 =

(31) 6 × 5 =

(32) 7 × 4 =

(33) 8 × 6 =

(34) 4 × 9 =

(35) 7 × 0 =

(36) 2 × 5 =

(37) 5 × 8 =

(38) 9 × 3 =

(39) 6 × 1 =

(40) 8 × 8 =

2 Multiply.

2 points per question

(1) $2 \times 7 =$

(2) $5 \times 3 =$

(3) $8 \times 5 =$

(4) $3 \times 9 =$

(5) $9 \times 9 =$

(6) $7 \times 7 =$

(7) $6 \times 4 =$

(8) $4 \times 6 =$

(9) $3 \times 3 =$

(10) $5 \times 5 =$

(11) $9 \times 8 =$

(12) $6 \times 3 =$

(13) $8 \times 1 =$

(14) $2 \times 2 =$

(15) $3 \times 4 =$

(16) $5 \times 6 =$

(17) $7 \times 2 =$

(18) $8 \times 7 =$

(19) $3 \times 5 =$

(20) $4 \times 7 =$

(21) $9 \times 1 =$

(22) $8 \times 4 =$

(23) $6 \times 2 =$

(24) $9 \times 7 =$

(25) $7 \times 5 =$

(26) $5 \times 2 =$

(27) $4 \times 4 =$

(28) $7 \times 8 =$

(29) $3 \times 0 =$

(30) $2 \times 1 =$

This is really tough - hang in there!

37

Date   /   /

Name

Score   /100

1 Multiply.

1 point per question

(1) $7 \times 1 =$

(2) $8 \times 4 =$

(3) $3 \times 9 =$

(4) $6 \times 5 =$

(5) $7 \times 7 =$

(6) $8 \times 7 =$

(7) $7 \times 5 =$

(8) $4 \times 8 =$

(9) $9 \times 7 =$

(10) $6 \times 8 =$

(11) $8 \times 6 =$

(12) $5 \times 7 =$

(13) $4 \times 9 =$

(14) $2 \times 6 =$

(15) $9 \times 7 =$

(16) $5 \times 1 =$

(17) $3 \times 8 =$

(18) $8 \times 9 =$

(19) $6 \times 7 =$

(20) $3 \times 5 =$

(21) $7 \times 2 =$

(22) $5 \times 4 =$

(23) $4 \times 3 =$

(24) $2 \times 9 =$

(25) $8 \times 8 =$

(26) $4 \times 7 =$

(27) $7 \times 9 =$

(28) $3 \times 7 =$

(29) $6 \times 1 =$

(30) $8 \times 5 =$

(31) $7 \times 7 =$

(32) $3 \times 4 =$

(33) $9 \times 2 =$

(34) $2 \times 0 =$

(35) $5 \times 3 =$

(36) $9 \times 8 =$

(37) $7 \times 9 =$

(38) $6 \times 9 =$

(39) $5 \times 5 =$

(40) $4 \times 2 =$

2 Multiply.

(1) $3 \times 6 =$

(2) $2 \times 7 =$

(3) $8 \times 2 =$

(4) $7 \times 5 =$

(5) $6 \times 3 =$

(6) $5 \times 8 =$

(7) $4 \times 4 =$

(8) $5 \times 6 =$

(9) $7 \times 6 =$

(10) $8 \times 7 =$

(11) $9 \times 3 =$

(12) $6 \times 2 =$

(13) $8 \times 1 =$

(14) $5 \times 9 =$

(15) $2 \times 5 =$

(16) $9 \times 9 =$

(17) $7 \times 4 =$

(18) $4 \times 5 =$

(19) $2 \times 8 =$

(20) $3 \times 3 =$

(21) $2 \times 4 =$

(22) $7 \times 9 =$

(23) $9 \times 5 =$

(24) $6 \times 6 =$

(25) $8 \times 3 =$

(26) $7 \times 2 =$

(27) $3 \times 2 =$

(28) $4 \times 0 =$

(29) $2 \times 5 =$

(30) $9 \times 6 =$

Are you remembering all of your times tables? Good job!

Level ★★

Date / / Name Score /100

1 Read each line from left to right. Then trace and write the correct values in this grid. Take the number on the side and multiply it by the number in the top row to get the correct value for each box.

25 points for completion

	2	3	4	5	6	7	8	9
2		6		10		14		18
3	6		12		18		24	
4		12		20		28		36
5	10		20		30		40	
6		18		30		42		54
7	14		28		42		56	
8	16	24	32	40	48	56	64	72
9	18	27	36	45	54	63	72	81

2 Fill in the missing numbers to complete this grid. Take the number on the side and multiply it by the number in the top row to get the correct value for each box.

25 points for completion

	2	3	4	5	6	7	8	9
2	4		8		12		16	
3		9		15		21		27
4	8		16		24		32	
5		15		25		35		45
6	12		24		36		48	
7		21		35		49		63
8	16		32		48		64	
9		27		45		63		81

3 **Fill in the missing numbers to complete this grid. Take the number on the side and multiply it by the number in the top row to get the correct value for each box.**

25 points for completion

×	2	3	4	5	6	7	8	9
2		6	8				16	18
3		9	12		18			27
4		12	16			28		36
5	10			25	30		40	
6	12		24		36	42		
7		21		35			56	63
8	16		32		48		64	
9	18	27				63		81

4 **Fill in the missing numbers to complete this grid. Take the number on the side and multiply it by the number in the top row to get the correct value for each box.**

25 points for completion

×	2	3	4	5	6	7	8	9
2	4							
3		9						
4			16					
5				25				
6					36			
7						49		
8							64	
9								81

Good job! Don't forget to check your answers.

Multiplication 1×

Date   /   /

Name

---

1 **Fill in the missing numbers in the boxes below.**

4 points per question

(1) 1 — 2 — 3 — 4 — ☐ — ☐ — ☐

(2) 2 — 3 — 4 — 5 — ☐ — ☐ — ☐

(3) 3 — 4 — 5 — 6 — ☐ — ☐ — ☐

(4) 4 — 5 — 6 — 7 — ☐ — ☐ — ☐

(5) 5 — 6 — 7 — 8 — ☐ — ☐ — ☐

---

2 **Trace the numbers while reading each sentence below. Then read the times table on the right.**

1 point per question

(1) 1 × 1 = 1
One times one is one.

(2) 1 × 2 = 2
One times two is two.

(3) 1 × 3 = 3
One times three is three.

(4) 1 × 4 = 4
One times four is four.

(5) 1 × 5 = 5
One times five is five.

(6) 1 × 6 = 6
One times six is six.

(7) 1 × 7 = 7
One times seven is seven.

(8) 1 × 8 = 8
One times eight is eight.

(9) 1 × 9 = 9
One times nine is nine.

Let's memorize!

The 1 × Table

1 × 1 = 1   One times one is one.

1 × 2 = 2   One times two is two.

1 × 3 = 3   One times three is three.

1 × 4 = 4   One times four is four.

1 × 5 = 5   One times five is five.

1 × 6 = 6   One times six is six.

1 × 7 = 7   One times seven is seven.

1 × 8 = 8   One times eight is eight.

1 × 9 = 9   One times nine is nine.

3 **Fill in the boxes while reading the number sentences below.**

2 points per question

(1) $1 \times 1 =$ ☐
One times one is one.

(2) $1 \times 2 =$ ☐
One times two is two.

(3) $1 \times 3 =$ ☐
One times three is three.

(4) $1 \times 4 =$ ☐
One times four is four.

(5) $1 \times 5 =$ ☐
One times five is five.

(6) $1 \times 6 =$ ☐
One times six is six.

(7) $1 \times 7 =$ ☐
One times seven is seven.

(8) $1 \times 8 =$ ☐
One times eight is eight.

(9) $1 \times 9 =$ ☐
One times nine is nine.

(10) $1 \times 4 =$ ☐
One times four is four.

4 **Multiply.**

3 points per question

(1) $1 \times 1 =$

(2) $1 \times 2 =$

(3) $1 \times 3 =$

(4) $1 \times 4 =$

(5) $1 \times 5 =$

(6) $1 \times 6 =$

(7) $1 \times 7 =$

(8) $1 \times 8 =$

(9) $1 \times 9 =$

(10) $1 \times 4 =$

(11) $1 \times 6 =$

(12) $1 \times 7 =$

(13) $1 \times 8 =$

(14) $1 \times 1 =$

(15) $1 \times 2 =$

(16) $1 \times 5 =$

(17) $1 \times 3 =$

Remember: One times a number is always the same number!

40

Multiplication 10×

Date / /

Name

Score /100

---

1 Fill in the missing numbers in the boxes below.

4 points per question

(1) 10 — 20 — 30 — 40 — ☐ — ☐ — ☐

(2) 20 — 30 — 40 — 50 — ☐ — ☐ — ☐

(3) 30 — 40 — 50 — 60 — ☐ — ☐ — ☐

(4) 40 — 50 — 60 — 70 — ☐ — ☐ — ☐

(5) 50 — 60 — 70 — 80 — ☐ — ☐ — ☐

---

2 Trace the numbers while reading each sentence below. Then read the times table on the right.

1 point per question

(1) 10 × 1 = 10
Ten times one is ten.

(2) 10 × 2 = 20
Ten times two is twenty.

(3) 10 × 3 = 30
Ten times three is thirty.

(4) 10 × 4 = 40
Ten times four is forty.

(5) 10 × 5 = 50
Ten times five is fifty.

(6) 10 × 6 = 60
Ten times six is sixty.

(7) 10 × 7 = 70
Ten times seven is seventy.

(8) 10 × 8 = 80
Ten times eight is eighty.

(9) 10 × 9 = 90
Ten times nine is ninety.

Let's memorize!

The 10× Table

10 × 1 = 10 Ten times one is ten.

10 × 2 = 20 Ten times two is twenty.

10 × 3 = 30 Ten times three is thirty.

10 × 4 = 40 Ten times four is forty.

10 × 5 = 50 Ten times five is fifty.

10 × 6 = 60 Ten times six is sixty.

10 × 7 = 70 Ten times seven is seventy.

10 × 8 = 80 Ten times eight is eighty.

10 × 9 = 90 Ten times nine is ninety.

③ Fill in the boxes while reading the number sentences below.

2 points per question

(1) $10 \times 1 = \boxed{}$
Ten times one is ten.

(2) $10 \times 2 = \boxed{}$
Ten times two is twenty.

(3) $10 \times 3 = \boxed{}$
Ten times three is thirty.

(4) $10 \times 4 = \boxed{}$
Ten times four is forty.

(5) $10 \times 5 = \boxed{}$
Ten times five is fifty.

(6) $10 \times 6 = \boxed{}$
Ten times six is sixty.

(7) $10 \times 7 = \boxed{}$
Ten times seven is seventy.

(8) $10 \times 8 = \boxed{}$
Ten times eight is eighty.

(9) $10 \times 9 = \boxed{}$
Ten times nine is ninety.

(10) $10 \times 4 = \boxed{}$
Ten times four is forty.

④ Multiply.

3 points per question

(1) $10 \times 1 =$

(2) $10 \times 2 =$

(3) $10 \times 3 =$

(4) $10 \times 4 =$

(5) $10 \times 5 =$

(6) $10 \times 6 =$

(7) $10 \times 7 =$

(8) $10 \times 8 =$

(9) $10 \times 9 =$

(10) $10 \times 4 =$

(11) $10 \times 6 =$

(12) $10 \times 7 =$

(13) $10 \times 8 =$

(14) $10 \times 1 =$

(15) $10 \times 2 =$

(16) $10 \times 5 =$

(17) $10 \times 3 =$

Way to work hard! You're almost done!

41 Review ◆Multiplication 1×, 10×

Level ★★★

Score

/100

Date   /   /

Name

1 Multiply.

2 points per question

(1) $1 \times 4 =$

(2) $1 \times 5 =$

(3) $1 \times 6 =$

(4) $10 \times 6 =$

(5) $10 \times 7 =$

(6) $10 \times 8 =$

(7) $10 \times 9 =$

(8) $1 \times 9 =$

(9) $1 \times 8 =$

(10) $1 \times 7 =$

(11) $1 \times 6 =$

(12) $10 \times 3 =$

(13) $10 \times 2 =$

(14) $10 \times 1 =$

(15) $1 \times 1 =$

(16) $1 \times 2 =$

(17) $1 \times 3 =$

(18) $10 \times 6 =$

(19) $10 \times 5 =$

(20) $10 \times 4 =$

2 Fill in the boxes below.

1 point per question

(1) $1 \times \boxed{} = 1$

(2) $1 \times \boxed{} = 2$

(3) $1 \times \boxed{} = 4$

(4) $10 \times \boxed{} = 20$

(5) $10 \times \boxed{} = 80$

(6) $10 \times \boxed{} = 40$

(7) $10 \times \boxed{} = 30$

(8) $10 \times \boxed{} = 60$

(9) $1 \times \boxed{} = 7$

(10) $1 \times \boxed{} = 9$

3 Multiply.

2 points per question

(1) $10 \times 5 =$

(2) $1 \times 0 =$

(3) $1 \times 2 =$

(4) $10 \times 8 =$

(5) $1 \times 1 =$

(6) $10 \times 4 =$

(7) $10 \times 9 =$

(8) $1 \times 6 =$

(9) $10 \times 3 =$

(10) $10 \times 7 =$

(11) $1 \times 4 =$

(12) $10 \times 0 =$

(13) $1 \times 5 =$

(14) $1 \times 8 =$

(15) $10 \times 2 =$

(16) $1 \times 9 =$

(17) $10 \times 1 =$

(18) $1 \times 3 =$

(19) $1 \times 7 =$

(20) $10 \times 6 =$

4 Fill in the boxes below.

1 point per question

(1) $1 \times \boxed{} = 3$

(2) $10 \times \boxed{} = 70$

(3) $1 \times \boxed{} = 5$

(4) $10 \times \boxed{} = 10$

(5) $10 \times \boxed{} = 90$

(6) $1 \times \boxed{} = 6$

(7) $10 \times \boxed{} = 0$

(8) $1 \times \boxed{} = 7$

(9) $10 \times \boxed{} = 50$

(10) $1 \times \boxed{} = 8$

Do you remember your ones and tens times tables?

Review ◆Commutative Property

Level ★★★

Date / /

Name

Score /100

1 Multiply.

2 points per question

(1) $2 \times 3 =$

(2) $3 \times 2 =$

(3) $3 \times 7 =$

(4) $7 \times 3 =$

(5) $4 \times 5 =$

(6) $5 \times 4 =$

(7) $3 \times 8 =$

(8) $8 \times 3 =$

(9) $6 \times 8 =$

(10) $8 \times 6 =$

(11) $1 \times 7 =$

(12) $7 \times 1 =$

Can you see how the answer is the same either way you order the numbers?
This is called the commutative property of multiplication!

2 Fill in the boxes below.

2 points per question

(1) $2 \times 3 = 3 \times \boxed{}$

(2) $3 \times 6 = 6 \times \boxed{}$

(3) $4 \times 7 = 7 \times \boxed{}$

(4) $6 \times 5 = \boxed{} \times 6$

(5) $3 \times 3 = \boxed{} \times 3$

(6) $8 \times 2 = \boxed{} \times 8$

(7) $3 \times 9 = 9 \times \boxed{}$

(8) $3 \times \boxed{} = 4 \times 3$

(9) $7 \times \boxed{} = 2 \times 7$

(10) $9 \times 3 = \boxed{} \times 9$

(11) $8 \times 1 = \boxed{} \times 8$

(12) $\boxed{} \times 2 = 2 \times 4$

(13) $\boxed{} \times 5 = 5 \times 6$

3 Multiply.

2 points per question

(1) $3 \times 5 =$

(2) $5 \times 3 =$

(3) $8 \times 4 =$

(4) $4 \times 8 =$

(5) $10 \times 5 =$

(6) $5 \times 10 =$

(7) $9 \times 1 =$

(8) $1 \times 9 =$

(9) $9 \times 8 =$

(10) $8 \times 9 =$

(11) $1 \times 10 =$

(12) $10 \times 1 =$

4 Fill in the boxes below.

2 points per question

(1) $6 \times 2 = 2 \times \boxed{}$

(2) $5 \times 9 = \boxed{} \times 5$

(3) $3 \times \boxed{} = 7 \times 3$

(4) $8 \times 7 = \boxed{} \times 8$

(5) $9 \times 3 = 3 \times \boxed{}$

(6) $8 \times 2 = \boxed{} \times 8$

(7) $10 \times 3 = 3 \times \boxed{}$

(8) $9 \times 8 = \boxed{} \times 9$

(9) $3 \times \boxed{} = 2 \times 3$

(10) $10 \times 4 = \boxed{} \times 10$

(11) $\boxed{} \times 2 = 2 \times 9$

(12) $7 \times \boxed{} = 5 \times 7$

(13) $\boxed{} \times 8 = 8 \times 6$

Easy, right? Good job!

85

Level ⭐⭐⭐

Score

/100

Date / /

Name

1 Multiply.

1 point per question

(1) $4 \times 3 =$

(2) $6 \times 6 =$

(3) $8 \times 2 =$

(4) $2 \times 7 =$

(5) $3 \times 0 =$

(6) $7 \times 8 =$

(7) $5 \times 1 =$

(8) $9 \times 4 =$

(9) $3 \times 9 =$

(10) $5 \times 4 =$

(11) $2 \times 2 =$

(12) $1 \times 7 =$

(13) $7 \times 0 =$

(14) $9 \times 3 =$

(15) $2 \times 5 =$

(16) $8 \times 9 =$

(17) $6 \times 2 =$

(18) $4 \times 8 =$

(19) $8 \times 1 =$

(20) $3 \times 4 =$

(21) $7 \times 6 =$

(22) $6 \times 9 =$

(23) $4 \times 5 =$

(24) $10 \times 9 =$

(25) $2 \times 6 =$

(26) $8 \times 7 =$

(27) $3 \times 8 =$

(28) $4 \times 1 =$

(29) $9 \times 9 =$

(30) $6 \times 3 =$

(31) $7 \times 4 =$

(32) $5 \times 6 =$

(33) $2 \times 0 =$

(34) $8 \times 5 =$

(35) $9 \times 6 =$

(36) $6 \times 8 =$

(37) $2 \times 9 =$

(38) $3 \times 3 =$

(39) $4 \times 7 =$

(40) $7 \times 1 =$

(41) $9 \times 2 =$

(42) $2 \times 4 =$

(43) $8 \times 0 =$

(44) $5 \times 3 =$

(45) $1 \times 5 =$

(46) $10 \times 6 =$

(47) $4 \times 4 =$

(48) $3 \times 1 =$

(49) $7 \times 3 =$

(50) $9 \times 1 =$

2 Multiply.

1 point per question

(1) $4 \times 2 =$

(2) $6 \times 7 =$

(3) $8 \times 4 =$

(4) $2 \times 8 =$

(5) $3 \times 6 =$

(6) $9 \times 8 =$

(7) $5 \times 2 =$

(8) $7 \times 9 =$

(9) $6 \times 5 =$

(10) $4 \times 9 =$

(11) $3 \times 1 =$

(12) $5 \times 5 =$

(13) $9 \times 7 =$

(14) $1 \times 8 =$

(15) $5 \times 8 =$

(16) $7 \times 2 =$

(17) $4 \times 6 =$

(18) $8 \times 3 =$

(19) $3 \times 7 =$

(20) $10 \times 7 =$

(21) $3 \times 5 =$

(22) $8 \times 8 =$

(23) $2 \times 3 =$

(24) $7 \times 5 =$

(25) $5 \times 9 =$

(26) $10 \times 4 =$

(27) $4 \times 0 =$

(28) $8 \times 6 =$

(29) $3 \times 2 =$

(30) $1 \times 3 =$

3 Fill in the boxes below.

2 points per question

(1) $3 \times 4 = 4 \times \boxed{}$

(2) $2 \times 8 = 8 \times \boxed{}$

(3) $5 \times 6 = 6 \times \boxed{}$

(4) $4 \times 8 = \boxed{} \times 4$

(5) $7 \times 7 = \boxed{} \times 7$

(6) $6 \times 3 = \boxed{} \times 6$

(7) $5 \times 9 = 9 \times \boxed{}$

(8) $2 \times \boxed{} = 7 \times 2$

(9) $8 \times \boxed{} = 3 \times 8$

(10) $9 \times 4 = \boxed{} \times 9$

Congratulations! You are ready for **Grade 3 Division**!

1 Repeated Addition
pp 2, 3

1
(1) 4   (5) 12
(2) 6   (6) 8
(3) 14   (7) 16
(4) 10   (8) 18

2
(1) 6   (4) 21
(2) 9   (5) 12
(3) 18   (6) 24

3
(1) 8   (3) 24
(2) 20   (4) 16

4
(1) 6
(2) 8
(3) 10
(4) 12
(5) 14
(6) 16
(7) 18
(8) 9
(9) 12
(10) 15
(11) 18
(12) 21
(13) 24
(14) 27

2 Repeated Addition
pp 4, 5

1
(1) 12
(2) 16
(3) 20
(4) 24
(5) 28
(6) 32
(7) 15
(8) 20
(9) 25
(10) 30
(11) 35
(12) 40

2
(1) 18
(2) 24
(3) 30
(4) 36
(5) 42
(6) 48
(7) 21
(8) 28
(9) 35
(10) 42
(11) 49
(12) 56
(13) 63

3 Repeated Addition
pp 6, 7

1
(1) 24
(2) 32
(3) 40
(4) 48
(5) 56
(6) 64
(7) 27
(8) 36
(9) 45
(10) 54
(11) 63
(12) 72

2
(1) 3
(2) 4
(3) 5
(4) 6
(5) 7

3
(1) 6
(2) 15
(3) 28
(4) 20
(5) 36
(6) 63
(7) 16
(8) 72

4 Review ◆Repeated Addition
pp 8, 9

1
(1) 9
(2) 20
(3) 16
(4) 35
(5) 10
(6) 18
(7) 35
(8) 12
(9) 40
(10) 6
(11) 15
(12) 25
(13) 54

2
(1) 24
(2) 30
(3) 27
(4) 14
(5) 24
(6) 20
(7) 28
(8) 12
(9) 40
(10) 81
(11) 49
(12) 48

5 Multiplication 2×
pp 10, 11

1
(1) 10 − 12 − 14
(2) 12 − 14 − 16
(3) 14 − 16 − 18
(4) 16 − 18 − 20
(5) 18 − 20 − 22

2 Advice
Was it difficult to trace the number sentences while reciting your 2× table? Make sure you know your 2× table well!

3
(1) 2   (6) 12
(2) 4   (7) 14
(3) 6   (8) 16
(4) 8   (9) 18
(5) 10   (10) 6

4
(1) 2   (7) 14   (13) 18
(2) 4   (8) 16   (14) 4
(3) 6   (9) 18   (15) 8
(4) 8   (10) 6   (16) 12
(5) 10   (11) 10   (17) 16
(6) 12   (12) 14

6 Multiplication 2×
pp 12, 13

1
(1) $2 \times 1 = 2$ (6) $2 \times 6 = 12$
(2) $2 \times 2 = 4$ (7) $2 \times 7 = 14$
(3) $2 \times 3 = 6$ (8) $2 \times 8 = 16$
(4) $2 \times 4 = 8$ (9) $2 \times 9 = 18$
(5) $2 \times 5 = 10$ (10) $2 \times 2 = 4$

2
(1) 10   (8) 14   (15) 18
(2) 12   (9) 16   (16) 16
(3) 14   (10) 18   (17) 14
(4) 2   (11) 8   (18) 12
(5) 4   (12) 6   (19) 10
(6) 6   (13) 4   (20) 8
(7) 8   (14) 2

③ (1) $2 \times 2 = 4$ (6) $2 \times 5 = 10$
(2) $2 \times 6 = 12$ (7) $2 \times 9 = 18$
(3) $2 \times 8 = 16$ (8) $2 \times 7 = 14$
(4) $2 \times 1 = 2$ (9) $2 \times 4 = 8$
(5) $2 \times 3 = 6$ (10) $2 \times 6 = 12$

④ (1) 4 (8) 14 (15) 14
(2) 8 (9) 18 (16) 10
(3) 12 (10) 16 (17) 6
(4) 16 (11) 12 (18) 2
(5) 2 (12) 8 (19) 18
(6) 6 (13) 4 (20) 16
(7) 10 (14) 18

⑦ Multiplication 2×
pp 14, 15

① (1) $2 \times 2 = 4$ (6) $2 \times 1 = 2$
(2) $2 \times 8 = 16$ (7) $2 \times 9 = 18$
(3) $2 \times 7 = 14$ (8) $2 \times 6 = 12$
(4) $2 \times 3 = 6$ (9) $2 \times 5 = 10$
(5) $2 \times 4 = 8$ (10) $2 \times 8 = 16$

② (1) 6 (8) 18 (15) 6
(2) 8 (9) 14 (16) 4
(3) 10 (10) 10 (17) 2
(4) 2 (11) 6 (18) 0
(5) 4 (12) 16 (19) 4
(6) 14 (13) 12 (20) 8
(7) 16 (14) 8

③ (1) 16 (8) 6 (15) 10
(2) 6 (9) 14 (16) 2
(3) 2 (10) 10 (17) 8
(4) 12 (11) 16 (18) 12
(5) 18 (12) 0 (19) 6
(6) 8 (13) 18 (20) 14
(7) 4 (14) 12

④ (1) 1 (6) 6
(2) 2 (7) 7
(3) 3 (8) 8
(4) 4 (9) 9
(5) 5 (10) 3

⑧ Multiplication 3×
pp 16, 17

① (1) $15 - 18 - 21$
(2) $18 - 21 - 24$
(3) $21 - 24 - 27$
(4) $24 - 27 - 30$
(5) $27 - 30 - 33$

② **Advice**

Did you enjoy tracing
the number sentences
while reciting your 3×
table? Make sure you
know your 3× table well!

③ (1) 3 (6) 18
(2) 6 (7) 21
(3) 9 (8) 24
(4) 12 (9) 27
(5) 15 (10) 12

④ (1) 3 (7) 21 (13) 27
(2) 6 (8) 24 (14) 6
(3) 9 (9) 27 (15) 12
(4) 12 (10) 9 (16) 18
(5) 15 (11) 15 (17) 24
(6) 18 (12) 21

⑨ Multiplication 3×
pp 18, 19

① (1) $3 \times 1 = 3$ (6) $3 \times 6 = 18$
(2) $3 \times 2 = 6$ (7) $3 \times 7 = 21$
(3) $3 \times 3 = 9$ (8) $3 \times 8 = 24$
(4) $3 \times 4 = 12$ (9) $3 \times 9 = 27$
(5) $3 \times 5 = 15$ (10) $3 \times 2 = 6$

② (1) 15 (8) 21 (15) 27
(2) 18 (9) 24 (16) 24
(3) 21 (10) 27 (17) 21
(4) 3 (11) 12 (18) 18
(5) 6 (12) 9 (19) 15
(6) 9 (13) 6 (20) 12
(7) 12 (14) 3

③ (1) $3 \times 2 = 6$ (6) $3 \times 7 = 21$
(2) $3 \times 6 = 18$ (7) $3 \times 9 = 27$
(3) $3 \times 8 = 24$ (8) $3 \times 5 = 15$
(4) $3 \times 1 = 3$ (9) $3 \times 4 = 12$
(5) $3 \times 3 = 9$ (10) $3 \times 6 = 18$

④ (1) 6 (8) 21 (15) 21
(2) 12 (9) 27 (16) 15
(3) 18 (10) 24 (17) 9
(4) 24 (11) 18 (18) 3
(5) 3 (12) 12 (19) 27
(6) 9 (13) 6 (20) 24
(7) 15 (14) 27

⑩ Multiplication 3×
pp 20, 21

① (1) $3 \times 5 = 15$ (6) $3 \times 7 = 21$
(2) $3 \times 3 = 9$ (7) $3 \times 6 = 18$
(3) $3 \times 8 = 24$ (8) $3 \times 1 = 3$
(4) $3 \times 2 = 6$ (9) $3 \times 4 = 12$
(5) $3 \times 9 = 27$ (10) $3 \times 8 = 24$

② (1) 9 (8) 27 (15) 9
(2) 12 (9) 21 (16) 6
(3) 15 (10) 15 (17) 3
(4) 3 (11) 9 (18) 0
(5) 6 (12) 24 (19) 6
(6) 21 (13) 18 (20) 12
(7) 24 (14) 12

③ (1) 24 (8) 9 (15) 15
(2) 9 (9) 21 (16) 3
(3) 3 (10) 15 (17) 12
(4) 18 (11) 24 (18) 18
(5) 27 (12) 0 (19) 9
(6) 12 (13) 27 (20) 21
(7) 6 (14) 18

④ (1) 1 (6) 6
(2) 2 (7) 7
(3) 3 (8) 8
(4) 4 (9) 9
(5) 5 (10) 3

11 Review ◆Multiplication 2×, 3× — pp 22, 23

1
(1) 8 (8) 18 (15) 2
(2) 10 (9) 16 (16) 4
(3) 12 (10) 14 (17) 6
(4) 18 (11) 12 (18) 18
(5) 21 (12) 9 (19) 15
(6) 24 (13) 6 (20) 12
(7) 27 (14) 3

2
(1) 3 (6) 9
(2) 4 (7) 8
(3) 5 (8) 7
(4) 1 (9) 6
(5) 2 (10) 5

3
(1) 15 (8) 12 (15) 6
(2) 0 (9) 9 (16) 18
(3) 4 (10) 21 (17) 3
(4) 24 (11) 8 (18) 6
(5) 2 (12) 0 (19) 14
(6) 12 (13) 10 (20) 18
(7) 27 (14) 16

4
(1) 6 (6) 0
(2) 3 (7) 2
(3) 1 (8) 9
(4) 8 (9) 7
(5) 9 (10) 4

12 Multiplication 4× — pp 24, 25

1
(1) 20 − 24 − 28
(2) 24 − 28 − 32
(3) 28 − 32 − 36
(4) 32 − 36 − 40
(5) 36 − 40 − 44

2 Advice
Was it difficult to trace
the number sentences
while reciting your 4×
table? Make sure you
know your 4× table well!

3
(1) 4 (6) 24
(2) 8 (7) 28
(3) 12 (8) 32
(4) 16 (9) 36
(5) 20 (10) 16

4
(1) 4 (7) 28 (13) 36
(2) 8 (8) 32 (14) 8
(3) 12 (9) 36 (15) 16
(4) 16 (10) 12 (16) 24
(5) 20 (11) 20 (17) 32
(6) 24 (12) 28

13 Multiplication 4× — pp 26, 27

1
(1) 4 × 1 = 4 (6) 4 × 6 = 24
(2) 4 × 2 = 8 (7) 4 × 7 = 28
(3) 4 × 3 = 12 (8) 4 × 8 = 32
(4) 4 × 4 = 16 (9) 4 × 9 = 36
(5) 4 × 5 = 20 (10) 4 × 6 = 24

2
(1) 20 (8) 28 (15) 36
(2) 24 (9) 32 (16) 32
(3) 28 (10) 36 (17) 28
(4) 4 (11) 16 (18) 24
(5) 8 (12) 12 (19) 20
(6) 12 (13) 8 (20) 16
(7) 16 (14) 4

3
(1) 4 × 3 = 12 (6) 4 × 9 = 36
(2) 4 × 6 = 24 (7) 4 × 4 = 16
(3) 4 × 8 = 32 (8) 4 × 7 = 28
(4) 4 × 2 = 8 (9) 4 × 5 = 20
(5) 4 × 1 = 4 (10) 4 × 6 = 24

4
(1) 8 (8) 28 (15) 28
(2) 16 (9) 36 (16) 20
(3) 24 (10) 32 (17) 12
(4) 32 (11) 24 (18) 4
(5) 4 (12) 16 (19) 16
(6) 12 (13) 8 (20) 32
(7) 20 (14) 36

14 Multiplication 4× — pp 28, 29

1
(1) 4 × 8 = 32 (6) 4 × 7 = 28
(2) 4 × 3 = 12 (7) 4 × 6 = 24
(3) 4 × 4 = 16 (8) 4 × 1 = 4
(4) 4 × 2 = 8 (9) 4 × 4 = 16
(5) 4 × 9 = 36 (10) 4 × 5 = 20

2
(1) 12 (8) 36 (15) 12
(2) 16 (9) 28 (16) 8
(3) 20 (10) 20 (17) 4
(4) 4 (11) 12 (18) 0
(5) 8 (12) 32 (19) 8
(6) 28 (13) 24 (20) 16
(7) 32 (14) 16

3
(1) 28 (8) 4 (15) 20
(2) 8 (9) 36 (16) 4
(3) 20 (10) 24 (17) 16
(4) 36 (11) 12 (18) 24
(5) 32 (12) 20 (19) 12
(6) 0 (13) 8 (20) 32
(7) 16 (14) 28

4
(1) 1 (6) 6
(2) 2 (7) 7
(3) 3 (8) 8
(4) 4 (9) 9
(5) 5 (10) 6

15 Multiplication 5× — pp 30, 31

1
(1) 25 − 30 − 35
(2) 30 − 35 − 40
(3) 35 − 40 − 45
(4) 40 − 45 − 50
(5) 45 − 50 − 55

2 Advice
Did you enjoy tracing
the number sentences
while reciting your 5×
table? Make sure you
know your 5× table well!

3
(1) 5 (6) 30
(2) 10 (7) 35
(3) 15 (8) 40
(4) 20 (9) 45
(5) 25 (10) 15

4
(1) 5 (7) 35 (13) 45
(2) 10 (8) 40 (14) 10
(3) 15 (9) 45 (15) 20
(4) 20 (10) 15 (16) 30
(5) 25 (11) 25 (17) 40
(6) 30 (12) 35

16 Multiplication 5×

pp 32, 33

1
(1) 5 × 1 = 5   (6) 5 × 6 = 30
(2) 5 × 2 = 10   (7) 5 × 7 = 35
(3) 5 × 3 = 15   (8) 5 × 8 = 40
(4) 5 × 4 = 20   (9) 5 × 9 = 45
(5) 5 × 5 = 25   (10) 5 × 3 = 15

2
(1) 25   (8) 35   (15) 45
(2) 30   (9) 40   (16) 40
(3) 35   (10) 45   (17) 35
(4) 5   (11) 20   (18) 30
(5) 10   (12) 15   (19) 25
(6) 15   (13) 10   (20) 20
(7) 20   (14) 5

3
(1) 5 × 2 = 10   (6) 5 × 7 = 35
(2) 5 × 6 = 30   (7) 5 × 9 = 45
(3) 5 × 8 = 40   (8) 5 × 5 = 25
(4) 5 × 1 = 5   (9) 5 × 4 = 20
(5) 5 × 3 = 15   (10) 5 × 6 = 30

4
(1) 10   (8) 35   (15) 35
(2) 20   (9) 45   (16) 25
(3) 30   (10) 40   (17) 15
(4) 40   (11) 30   (18) 5
(5) 5   (12) 20   (19) 20
(6) 15   (13) 10   (20) 40
(7) 25   (14) 45

17 Multiplication 5×

pp 34, 35

1
(1) 5 × 8 = 40   (6) 5 × 7 = 35
(2) 5 × 3 = 15   (7) 5 × 6 = 30
(3) 5 × 4 = 20   (8) 5 × 1 = 5
(4) 5 × 2 = 10   (9) 5 × 4 = 20
(5) 5 × 9 = 45   (10) 5 × 5 = 25

2
(1) 15   (8) 45   (15) 15
(2) 20   (9) 35   (16) 10
(3) 25   (10) 25   (17) 5
(4) 5   (11) 15   (18) 0
(5) 10   (12) 40   (19) 10
(6) 35   (13) 30   (20) 20
(7) 40   (14) 20

3
(1) 35   (8) 5   (15) 25
(2) 10   (9) 45   (16) 5
(3) 25   (10) 30   (17) 20
(4) 45   (11) 15   (18) 30
(5) 40   (12) 25   (19) 15
(6) 0   (13) 10   (20) 40
(7) 20   (14) 35

4
(1) 1   (6) 6
(2) 2   (7) 7
(3) 3   (8) 8
(4) 4   (9) 9
(5) 5   (10) 3

18 Review ◆Multiplication 4×, 5×

pp 36, 37

1
(1) 16   (8) 36   (15) 4
(2) 20   (9) 32   (16) 8
(3) 24   (10) 28   (17) 12
(4) 30   (11) 24   (18) 30
(5) 35   (12) 15   (19) 25
(6) 40   (13) 10   (20) 20
(7) 45   (14) 5

2
(1) 3   (6) 9
(2) 4   (7) 8
(3) 5   (8) 7
(4) 1   (9) 6
(5) 2   (10) 5

3
(1) 20   (8) 30   (15) 8
(2) 0   (9) 12   (16) 45
(3) 10   (10) 28   (17) 4
(4) 32   (11) 20   (18) 15
(5) 5   (12) 0   (19) 35
(6) 16   (13) 25   (20) 24
(7) 36   (14) 40

4
(1) 6   (6) 4
(2) 3   (7) 2
(3) 1   (8) 0
(4) 8   (9) 7
(5) 9   (10) 9

19 Review ◆Multiplication 2× to 5×

pp 38, 39

1
(1) 4   (11) 18   (21) 30
(2) 8   (12) 24   (22) 20
(3) 12   (13) 8   (23) 45
(4) 10   (14) 16   (24) 35
(5) 14   (15) 24   (25) 25
(6) 18   (16) 32   (26) 6
(7) 9   (17) 20   (27) 12
(8) 15   (18) 28   (28) 20
(9) 21   (19) 36   (29) 5
(10) 12   (20) 40   (30) 16

2
(1) 18   (8) 10   (15) 16
(2) 24   (9) 21   (16) 24
(3) 28   (10) 20   (17) 35
(4) 30   (11) 6   (18) 32
(5) 10   (12) 16   (19) 27
(6) 12   (13) 0   (20) 12
(7) 12   (14) 45

3

	2	3	4	5	6	7	8	9
2	4	6	8	10	12	14	16	18
3	6	9	12	15	18	21	24	27
4	8	12	16	20	24	28	32	36
5	10	15	20	25	30	35	40	45

4

	2	3	4	5	6	7	8	9
2	4	6	8	10	12	14	16	18
3	6	9	12	15	18	21	24	27
4	8	12	16	20	24	28	32	36
5	10	15	20	25	30	35	40	45

20 Multiplication 6×

pp 40, 41

1
(1) 30 – 36 – 42
(2) 36 – 42 – 48
(3) 42 – 48 – 54
(4) 48 – 54 – 60
(5) 54 – 60 – 66

2 Advice
Do you think the 6× table is very hard? Work hard, and make sure you know your 6× table well!

3
(1) 6   (6) 36
(2) 12   (7) 42
(3) 18   (8) 48
(4) 24   (9) 54
(5) 30   (10) 24

4
(1) 6   (7) 42   (13) 54
(2) 12   (8) 48   (14) 12
(3) 18   (9) 54   (15) 24
(4) 24   (10) 18   (16) 36
(5) 30   (11) 30   (17) 48
(6) 36   (12) 42

(21) Multiplication 6×

pp 42, 43

1
(1) 6 × 1 = 6   (6) 6 × 6 = 36
(2) 6 × 2 = 12   (7) 6 × 7 = 42
(3) 6 × 3 = 18   (8) 6 × 8 = 48
(4) 6 × 4 = 24   (9) 6 × 9 = 54
(5) 6 × 5 = 30   (10) 6 × 6 = 36

2
(1) 30   (8) 42   (15) 54
(2) 36   (9) 48   (16) 48
(3) 42   (10) 54   (17) 42
(4) 6   (11) 24   (18) 36
(5) 12   (12) 18   (19) 30
(6) 18   (13) 12   (20) 24
(7) 24   (14) 6

3
(1) 6 × 3 = 18   (6) 6 × 8 = 48
(2) 6 × 6 = 36   (7) 6 × 9 = 54
(3) 6 × 7 = 42   (8) 6 × 5 = 30
(4) 6 × 1 = 6   (9) 6 × 4 = 24
(5) 6 × 2 = 12   (10) 6 × 3 = 18

4
(1) 12   (8) 42   (15) 42
(2) 24   (9) 54   (16) 30
(3) 36   (10) 48   (17) 18
(4) 48   (11) 36   (18) 6
(5) 6   (12) 24   (19) 24
(6) 18   (13) 12   (20) 48
(7) 30   (14) 54

(22) Multiplication 6×

pp 44, 45

1
(1) 6 × 4 = 24   (6) 6 × 5 = 30
(2) 6 × 8 = 48   (7) 6 × 9 = 54
(3) 6 × 6 = 36   (8) 6 × 7 = 42
(4) 6 × 2 = 12   (9) 6 × 1 = 6
(5) 6 × 3 = 18   (10) 6 × 8 = 48

2
(1) 18   (8) 54   (15) 18
(2) 24   (9) 42   (16) 12
(3) 30   (10) 30   (17) 6
(4) 6   (11) 18   (18) 0
(5) 12   (12) 48   (19) 12
(6) 42   (13) 36   (20) 24
(7) 48   (14) 24

3
(1) 42   (8) 6   (15) 30
(2) 12   (9) 54   (16) 6
(3) 30   (10) 36   (17) 24
(4) 54   (11) 18   (18) 36
(5) 48   (12) 30   (19) 18
(6) 0   (13) 12   (20) 48
(7) 24   (14) 42

4
(1) 1   (6) 6
(2) 2   (7) 7
(3) 3   (8) 8
(4) 4   (9) 9
(5) 5   (10) 3

(23) Multiplication 7×

pp 46, 47

1
(1) 35 − 42 − 49
(2) 42 − 49 − 56
(3) 49 − 56 − 63
(4) 56 − 63 − 70
(5) 63 − 70 − 77

2 Advice
Was it difficult to trace the number sentences while reciting your 7× table? Make sure you know your 7× table well!

3
(1) 7   (6) 42
(2) 14   (7) 49
(3) 21   (8) 56
(4) 28   (9) 63
(5) 35   (10) 28

4
(1) 7   (7) 49   (13) 63
(2) 14   (8) 56   (14) 14
(3) 21   (9) 63   (15) 28
(4) 28   (10) 21   (16) 42
(5) 35   (11) 35   (17) 56
(6) 42   (12) 49

(24) Multiplication 7×

pp 48, 49

1
(1) 7 × 1 = 7   (6) 7 × 6 = 42
(2) 7 × 2 = 14   (7) 7 × 7 = 49
(3) 7 × 3 = 21   (8) 7 × 8 = 56
(4) 7 × 4 = 28   (9) 7 × 9 = 63
(5) 7 × 5 = 35   (10) 7 × 4 = 28

2
(1) 35   (8) 49   (15) 63
(2) 42   (9) 56   (16) 56
(3) 49   (10) 63   (17) 49
(4) 7   (11) 28   (18) 42
(5) 14   (12) 21   (19) 35
(6) 21   (13) 14   (20) 28
(7) 28   (14) 7

3
(1) 7 × 2 = 14   (6) 7 × 7 = 49
(2) 7 × 6 = 42   (7) 7 × 9 = 63
(3) 7 × 8 = 56   (8) 7 × 5 = 35
(4) 7 × 1 = 7   (9) 7 × 4 = 28
(5) 7 × 3 = 21   (10) 7 × 8 = 56

4
(1) 14   (8) 49   (15) 49
(2) 28   (9) 63   (16) 35
(3) 42   (10) 56   (17) 21
(4) 56   (11) 42   (18) 7
(5) 7   (12) 28   (19) 28
(6) 21   (13) 14   (20) 56
(7) 35   (14) 63

(25) Multiplication 7×

pp 50, 51

1
(1) 7 × 5 = 35   (6) 7 × 7 = 49
(2) 7 × 3 = 21   (7) 7 × 6 = 42
(3) 7 × 4 = 28   (8) 7 × 1 = 7
(4) 7 × 2 = 14   (9) 7 × 8 = 56
(5) 7 × 9 = 63   (10) 7 × 5 = 35

2
(1) 21 (8) 63 (15) 21
(2) 28 (9) 49 (16) 14
(3) 35 (10) 35 (17) 7
(4) 7 (11) 21 (18) 0
(5) 14 (12) 56 (19) 14
(6) 49 (13) 42 (20) 28
(7) 56 (14) 28

3
(1) 49 (8) 7 (15) 35
(2) 14 (9) 63 (16) 7
(3) 35 (10) 42 (17) 28
(4) 63 (11) 21 (18) 42
(5) 56 (12) 35 (19) 21
(6) 0 (13) 14 (20) 56
(7) 28 (14) 49

4
(1) 1 (6) 6
(2) 2 (7) 7
(3) 3 (8) 8
(4) 4 (9) 9
(5) 5 (10) 4

3

×	2	3	4	5	6	7	8	9
2	4	6	8	10	12	14	16	18
3	6	9	12	15	18	21	24	27
4	8	12	16	20	24	28	32	36
5	10	15	20	25	30	35	40	45
6	12	18	24	30	36	42	48	54
7	14	21	28	35	42	49	56	63

4

×	2	3	4	5	6	7	8	9
2	4	6	8	10	12	14	16	18
3	6	9	12	15	18	21	24	27
4	8	12	16	20	24	28	32	36
5	10	15	20	25	30	35	40	45
6	12	18	24	30	36	42	48	54
7	14	21	28	35	42	49	56	63

26 Review ◆Multiplication 6×, 7×　　pp 52, 53

1
(1) 24 (8) 54 (15) 6
(2) 30 (9) 48 (16) 12
(3) 36 (10) 42 (17) 18
(4) 42 (11) 36 (18) 42
(5) 49 (12) 21 (19) 35
(6) 56 (13) 14 (20) 28
(7) 63 (14) 7

2
(1) 3 (6) 9
(2) 4 (7) 8
(3) 5 (8) 7
(4) 1 (9) 6
(5) 2 (10) 5

3
(1) 35 (8) 36 (15) 14
(2) 0 (9) 21 (16) 54
(3) 12 (10) 49 (17) 7
(4) 56 (11) 24 (18) 18
(5) 6 (12) 0 (19) 42
(6) 28 (13) 30 (20) 42
(7) 63 (14) 48

4
(1) 6 (6) 4
(2) 8 (7) 2
(3) 1 (8) 0
(4) 3 (9) 7
(5) 9 (10) 9

27 Review ◆Multiplication 2× to 7×　　pp 54, 55

1
(1) 18 (16) 15 (31) 56
(2) 14 (17) 12 (32) 12
(3) 10 (18) 24 (33) 28
(4) 6 (19) 36 (34) 18
(5) 24 (20) 48 (35) 15
(6) 18 (21) 7 (36) 20
(7) 12 (22) 21 (37) 42
(8) 6 (23) 35 (38) 8
(9) 32 (24) 49 (39) 40
(10) 24 (25) 63 (40) 21
(11) 16 (26) 16 (41) 30
(12) 8 (27) 9 (42) 4
(13) 45 (28) 36 (43) 27
(14) 35 (29) 10 (44) 30
(15) 25 (30) 6 (45) 28

2
(1) 14 (6) 28 (11) 45
(2) 6 (7) 12 (12) 21
(3) 32 (8) 12 (13) 0
(4) 25 (9) 42 (14) 20
(5) 54 (10) 3 (15) 18

28 Multiplication 8×　　pp 56, 57

1
(1) 40 − 48 − 56
(2) 48 − 56 − 64
(3) 56 − 64 − 72
(4) 64 − 72 − 80
(5) 72 − 80 − 88

2 Advice
The 8× table can be very difficult. Keep practicing and make sure you know your 8× table well!

3
(1) 8 (6) 48
(2) 16 (7) 56
(3) 24 (8) 64
(4) 32 (9) 72
(5) 40 (10) 32

4
(1) 8 (7) 56 (13) 72
(2) 16 (8) 64 (14) 16
(3) 24 (9) 72 (15) 32
(4) 32 (10) 24 (16) 48
(5) 40 (11) 40 (17) 64
(6) 48 (12) 56

29 Multiplication 8×　　pp 58, 59

1
(1) $8 \times 1 = 8$ (6) $8 \times 6 = 48$
(2) $8 \times 2 = 16$ (7) $8 \times 7 = 56$
(3) $8 \times 3 = 24$ (8) $8 \times 8 = 64$
(4) $8 \times 4 = 32$ (9) $8 \times 9 = 72$
(5) $8 \times 5 = 40$ (10) $8 \times 4 = 32$

2
(1) 40 (8) 56 (15) 72
(2) 48 (9) 64 (16) 64
(3) 56 (10) 72 (17) 56
(4) 8 (11) 32 (18) 48
(5) 16 (12) 24 (19) 40
(6) 24 (13) 16 (20) 32
(7) 32 (14) 8

3
(1) $8 \times 3 = 24$ (6) $8 \times 7 = 56$
(2) $8 \times 6 = 48$ (7) $8 \times 5 = 40$
(3) $8 \times 8 = 64$ (8) $8 \times 4 = 32$
(4) $8 \times 2 = 16$ (9) $8 \times 9 = 72$
(5) $8 \times 1 = 8$ (10) $8 \times 8 = 64$

4
(1) 16 (8) 56 (15) 56
(2) 32 (9) 72 (16) 40
(3) 48 (10) 64 (17) 24
(4) 64 (11) 48 (18) 8
(5) 8 (12) 32 (19) 32
(6) 24 (13) 16 (20) 64
(7) 40 (14) 72

(30) Multiplication 8× pp 60,61

1
(1) $8 \times 3 = 24$ (6) $8 \times 7 = 56$
(2) $8 \times 6 = 48$ (7) $8 \times 9 = 72$
(3) $8 \times 5 = 40$ (8) $8 \times 8 = 64$
(4) $8 \times 2 = 16$ (9) $8 \times 4 = 32$
(5) $8 \times 1 = 8$ (10) $8 \times 3 = 24$

2
(1) 24 (8) 72 (15) 24
(2) 32 (9) 56 (16) 16
(3) 40 (10) 40 (17) 8
(4) 8 (11) 24 (18) 0
(5) 16 (12) 64 (19) 16
(6) 56 (13) 48 (20) 32
(7) 64 (14) 32

3
(1) 56 (8) 8 (15) 40
(2) 16 (9) 72 (16) 8
(3) 40 (10) 48 (17) 32
(4) 72 (11) 24 (18) 48
(5) 64 (12) 40 (19) 24
(6) 0 (13) 16 (20) 64
(7) 32 (14) 56

4
(1) 1 (6) 6
(2) 2 (7) 7
(3) 3 (8) 8
(4) 4 (9) 9
(5) 5 (10) 4

(31) Multiplication 9× pp 62,63

1
(1) 45 − 54 − 63
(2) 54 − 63 − 72
(3) 63 − 72 − 81
(4) 72 − 81 − 90
(5) 81 − 90 − 99

2 Advice
Wow, the 9× table looks very hard. Make sure you memorize it, so that you know your 9× table well!

3
(1) 9 (6) 54
(2) 18 (7) 63
(3) 27 (8) 72
(4) 36 (9) 81
(5) 45 (10) 36

4
(1) 9 (7) 63 (13) 81
(2) 18 (8) 72 (14) 18
(3) 27 (9) 81 (15) 36
(4) 36 (10) 27 (16) 54
(5) 45 (11) 45 (17) 72
(6) 54 (12) 63

(32) Multiplication 9× pp 64,65

1
(1) $9 \times 1 = 9$ (6) $9 \times 6 = 54$
(2) $9 \times 2 = 18$ (7) $9 \times 7 = 63$
(3) $9 \times 3 = 27$ (8) $9 \times 8 = 72$
(4) $9 \times 4 = 36$ (9) $9 \times 9 = 81$
(5) $9 \times 5 = 45$ (10) $9 \times 6 = 54$

2
(1) 45 (8) 63 (15) 81
(2) 54 (9) 72 (16) 72
(3) 63 (10) 81 (17) 63
(4) 9 (11) 36 (18) 54
(5) 18 (12) 27 (19) 45
(6) 27 (13) 18 (20) 36
(7) 36 (14) 9

3
(1) $9 \times 2 = 18$ (6) $9 \times 1 = 9$
(2) $9 \times 6 = 54$ (7) $9 \times 8 = 72$
(3) $9 \times 3 = 27$ (8) $9 \times 5 = 45$
(4) $9 \times 7 = 63$ (9) $9 \times 4 = 36$
(5) $9 \times 9 = 81$ (10) $9 \times 3 = 27$

4
(1) 18 (8) 63 (15) 63
(2) 36 (9) 81 (16) 45
(3) 54 (10) 72 (17) 27
(4) 72 (11) 54 (18) 9
(5) 9 (12) 36 (19) 36
(6) 27 (13) 18 (20) 54
(7) 45 (14) 81

(33) Multiplication 9× pp 66,67

1
(1) $9 \times 3 = 27$ (6) $9 \times 8 = 72$
(2) $9 \times 5 = 45$ (7) $9 \times 9 = 81$
(3) $9 \times 6 = 54$ (8) $9 \times 7 = 63$
(4) $9 \times 2 = 18$ (9) $9 \times 1 = 9$
(5) $9 \times 4 = 36$ (10) $9 \times 5 = 45$

2
(1) 27 (8) 81 (15) 27
(2) 36 (9) 63 (16) 18
(3) 45 (10) 45 (17) 9
(4) 9 (11) 27 (18) 0
(5) 18 (12) 72 (19) 18
(6) 63 (13) 54 (20) 36
(7) 72 (14) 36

3
(1) 63 (8) 9 (15) 45
(2) 18 (9) 81 (16) 9
(3) 45 (10) 54 (17) 36
(4) 81 (11) 27 (18) 54
(5) 72 (12) 45 (19) 27
(6) 0 (13) 18 (20) 72
(7) 36 (14) 63

4
(1) 1 (6) 6
(2) 2 (7) 7
(3) 3 (8) 8
(4) 4 (9) 9
(5) 5 (10) 2

34 Review ◆Multiplication 8×, 9×   pp 68,69

1
(1) 32	(8) 72	(15) 8
(2) 40	(9) 64	(16) 16
(3) 48	(10) 56	(17) 24
(4) 54	(11) 48	(18) 54
(5) 63	(12) 27	(19) 45
(6) 72	(13) 18	(20) 36
(7) 81	(14) 9	

2
(1) 1	(6) 7
(2) 2	(7) 6
(3) 5	(8) 9
(4) 4	(9) 5
(5) 3	(10) 8

3
(1) 45	(8) 48	(15) 18
(2) 0	(9) 27	(16) 72
(3) 16	(10) 63	(17) 9
(4) 72	(11) 32	(18) 24
(5) 8	(12) 0	(19) 56
(6) 36	(13) 40	(20) 54
(7) 81	(14) 64	

4
(1) 6	(6) 4
(2) 3	(7) 7
(3) 9	(8) 0
(4) 8	(9) 2
(5) 1	(10) 9

35 Review ◆Multiplication 2× to 9×   pp 70,71

1
(1) 6	(15) 28	(29) 21
(2) 14	(16) 42	(30) 32
(3) 12	(17) 56	(31) 24
(4) 27	(18) 24	(32) 16
(5) 12	(19) 40	(33) 45
(6) 20	(20) 56	(34) 35
(7) 28	(21) 72	(35) 25
(8) 20	(22) 18	(36) 24
(9) 30	(23) 36	(37) 36
(10) 40	(24) 54	(38) 48
(11) 18	(25) 72	(39) 21
(12) 30	(26) 8	(40) 35
(13) 42	(27) 16	
(14) 14	(28) 9	

2
(1) 10	(11) 63	(21) 21
(2) 6	(12) 45	(22) 4
(3) 32	(13) 2	(23) 81
(4) 15	(14) 4	(24) 10
(5) 54	(15) 12	(25) 64
(6) 49	(16) 32	(26) 18
(7) 16	(17) 24	(27) 6
(8) 54	(18) 24	(28) 15
(9) 18	(19) 48	(29) 27
(10) 5	(20) 8	(30) 12

36 Review ◆Multiplication 2× to 9×   pp 72,73

1
(1) 6	(15) 16	(29) 32
(2) 32	(16) 15	(30) 18
(3) 54	(17) 24	(31) 30
(4) 40	(18) 24	(32) 28
(5) 6	(19) 54	(33) 48
(6) 35	(20) 45	(34) 36
(7) 42	(21) 8	(35) 0
(8) 36	(22) 63	(36) 10
(9) 21	(23) 8	(37) 40
(10) 16	(24) 42	(38) 27
(11) 63	(25) 45	(39) 6
(12) 12	(26) 21	(40) 64
(13) 20	(27) 20	
(14) 36	(28) 5	

2
(1) 14	(11) 72	(21) 9
(2) 15	(12) 18	(22) 32
(3) 40	(13) 8	(23) 12
(4) 27	(14) 4	(24) 63
(5) 81	(15) 12	(25) 35
(6) 49	(16) 30	(26) 10
(7) 24	(17) 14	(27) 16
(8) 24	(18) 56	(28) 56
(9) 9	(19) 15	(29) 0
(10) 25	(20) 28	(30) 2

37 Review ◆Multiplication 2× to 9×   pp 74,75

1
(1) 7	(15) 63	(29) 6
(2) 32	(16) 5	(30) 40
(3) 27	(17) 24	(31) 49
(4) 30	(18) 72	(32) 12
(5) 49	(19) 42	(33) 18
(6) 56	(20) 15	(34) 0
(7) 35	(21) 14	(35) 15
(8) 32	(22) 20	(36) 72
(9) 63	(23) 12	(37) 63
(10) 48	(24) 18	(38) 54
(11) 48	(25) 64	(39) 25
(12) 35	(26) 28	(40) 8
(13) 36	(27) 63	
(14) 12	(28) 21	

2
(1) 18	(11) 27	(21) 8
(2) 14	(12) 12	(22) 63
(3) 16	(13) 8	(23) 45
(4) 35	(14) 45	(24) 36
(5) 18	(15) 10	(25) 24
(6) 40	(16) 81	(26) 14
(7) 16	(17) 28	(27) 6
(8) 30	(18) 20	(28) 0
(9) 42	(19) 16	(29) 10
(10) 56	(20) 9	(30) 54

38 Review ◆Multiplication 2× to 9×   pp 76,77

1
×	2	3	4	5	6	7	8	9
2	4	6	8	10	12	14	16	18
3	6	9	12	15	18	21	24	27
4	8	12	16	20	24	28	32	36
5	10	15	20	25	30	35	40	45
6	12	18	24	30	36	42	48	54
7	14	21	28	35	42	49	56	63
8	16	24	32	40	48	56	64	72
9	18	27	36	45	54	63	72	81

2
×	2	3	4	5	6	7	8	9
2	4	6	8	10	12	14	16	18
3	6	9	12	15	18	21	24	27
4	8	12	16	20	24	28	32	36
5	10	15	20	25	30	35	40	45
6	12	18	24	30	36	42	48	54
7	14	21	28	35	42	49	56	63
8	16	24	32	40	48	56	64	72
9	18	27	36	45	54	63	72	81

3
×	2	3	4	5	6	7	8	9
2	4	6	8	10	12	14	16	18
3	6	9	12	15	18	21	24	27
4	8	12	16	20	24	28	32	36
5	10	15	20	25	30	35	40	45
6	12	18	24	30	36	42	48	54
7	14	21	28	35	42	49	56	63
8	16	24	32	40	48	56	64	72
9	18	27	36	45	54	63	72	81

④	2	3	4	5	6	7	8	9
2	4	6	8	10	12	14	16	18
3	6	9	12	15	18	21	24	27
4	8	12	16	20	24	28	32	36
5	10	15	20	25	30	35	40	45
6	12	18	24	30	36	42	48	54
7	14	21	28	35	42	49	56	63
8	16	24	32	40	48	56	64	72
9	18	27	36	45	54	63	72	81

(39) Multiplication 1×

pp 78, 79

1
(1) 5 − 6 − 7
(2) 6 − 7 − 8
(3) 7 − 8 − 9
(4) 8 − 9 − 10
(5) 9 − 10 − 11

2 Advice
1 times a number is the same number! Easy, right?

3
(1) 1　(6) 6
(2) 2　(7) 7
(3) 3　(8) 8
(4) 4　(9) 9
(5) 5　(10) 4

4
(1) 1　(7) 7　(13) 8
(2) 2　(8) 8　(14) 1
(3) 3　(9) 9　(15) 2
(4) 4　(10) 4　(16) 5
(5) 5　(11) 6　(17) 3
(6) 6　(12) 7

(40) Multiplication 10×

pp 80, 81

1
(1) 50 − 60 − 70
(2) 60 − 70 − 80
(3) 70 − 80 − 90
(4) 80 − 90 − 100
(5) 90 − 100 − 110

2 Advice
Was it difficult to trace the number sentences while you were reading the 10× table?

3
(1) 10　(6) 60
(2) 20　(7) 70
(3) 30　(8) 80
(4) 40　(9) 90
(5) 50　(10) 40

4
(1) 10　(7) 70　(13) 80
(2) 20　(8) 80　(14) 10
(3) 30　(9) 90　(15) 20
(4) 40　(10) 40　(16) 50
(5) 50　(11) 60　(17) 30
(6) 60　(12) 70

(41) Review ◆Multiplication 1×, 10×

pp 82, 83

1
(1) 4　(8) 9　(15) 1
(2) 5　(9) 8　(16) 2
(3) 6　(10) 7　(17) 3
(4) 60　(11) 6　(18) 60
(5) 70　(12) 30　(19) 50
(6) 80　(13) 20　(20) 40
(7) 90　(14) 10

2
(1) 1　(6) 4
(2) 2　(7) 3
(3) 4　(8) 6
(4) 2　(9) 7
(5) 8　(10) 9

3
(1) 50　(8) 6　(15) 20
(2) 0　(9) 30　(16) 9
(3) 2　(10) 70　(17) 10
(4) 80　(11) 4　(18) 3
(5) 1　(12) 0　(19) 7
(6) 40　(13) 5　(20) 60
(7) 90　(14) 8

4
(1) 3　(6) 6
(2) 7　(7) 0
(3) 5　(8) 7
(4) 1　(9) 5
(5) 9　(10) 8

(42) Review ◆Commutative Property

pp 84, 85

1
(1) 6　(7) 24
(2) 6　(8) 24
(3) 21　(9) 48
(4) 21　(10) 48
(5) 20　(11) 7
(6) 20　(12) 7

2
(1) 2　(6) 2　(11) 1
(2) 3　(7) 3　(12) 4
(3) 4　(8) 4　(13) 6
(4) 5　(9) 2
(5) 3　(10) 3

3
(1) 15　(5) 50　(9) 72
(2) 15　(6) 50　(10) 72
(3) 32　(7) 9　(11) 10
(4) 32　(8) 9　(12) 10

4
(1) 6　(6) 2　(11) 9
(2) 9　(7) 10　(12) 5
(3) 7　(8) 8　(13) 6
(4) 7　(9) 2
(5) 9　(10) 4

(43) Review

pp 86, 87

1
(1) 12　(18) 32　(35) 54
(2) 36　(19) 8　(36) 48
(3) 16　(20) 12　(37) 18
(4) 14　(21) 42　(38) 9
(5) 0　(22) 54　(39) 28
(6) 56　(23) 20　(40) 7
(7) 5　(24) 90　(41) 18
(8) 36　(25) 12　(42) 8
(9) 27　(26) 56　(43) 0
(10) 20　(27) 24　(44) 15
(11) 4　(28) 4　(45) 5
(12) 7　(29) 81　(46) 60
(13) 0　(30) 18　(47) 16
(14) 27　(31) 28　(48) 3
(15) 10　(32) 30　(49) 21
(16) 72　(33) 0　(50) 9
(17) 12　(34) 40

2
(1) 8　(11) 3　(21) 15
(2) 42　(12) 25　(22) 64
(3) 32　(13) 63　(23) 6
(4) 16　(14) 8　(24) 35
(5) 18　(15) 40　(25) 45
(6) 72　(16) 14　(26) 40
(7) 10　(17) 24　(27) 0
(8) 63　(18) 24　(28) 48
(9) 30　(19) 21　(29) 6
(10) 36　(20) 70　(30) 3

3
(1) 3　(6) 3
(2) 2　(7) 5
(3) 5　(8) 7
(4) 8　(9) 3
(5) 7　(10) 4

Advice
If you made many mistakes in ① or ②, start reviewing on page 10.
If you made many mistakes in ③, start reviewing on page 84.